Introduction to Problem Solving

Grades PreK–2

Other Books in The Math Process Standards Series

Introduction to Reasoning and Proof: Grades PreK–2
(Schultz-Ferrell, Hammond, and Robles)
Introduction to Communication: Grades PreK–2 (O'Connell and O'Connor)
Introduction to Connections: Grades PreK–2 (Bamberger and Oberdorf)
Introduction to Represenation: Grades PreK–2 (Witeck and Ennis)

For information on the 3–5 grades and 6–8 grades series see the Heinemann website, www.heinemann.com.

Introduction to Problem Solving

Grades PreK–2

Susan O'Connell

The Math Process Standards Series
Susan O'Connell, Series Editor

HEINEMANN
Portsmouth, NH

Heinemann
A division of Reed Elsevier Inc.
361 Hanover Street
Portsmouth, NH 03801–3912
www.heinemann.com

Offices and agents throughout the world

The author and publisher wish to thank those who have generously given permission to reprint borrowed material:

Excerpts from *Principles and Standards for School Mathematics*. Copyright © 2000 by the National Council of Teachers of Mathematics. Reprinted with permission. All rights reserved.

Library of Congress Cataloging-in-Publication Data
O'Connell, Susan.
    Introduction to problem solving : grades preK–2 / Susan O'Connell.
        p. cm. — (The math process standards series)
    Includes bibliographical references.
    ISBN 978-0-325-01105-9 (alk. paper)
    1. Problem solving—Study and teaching (Elementary).   2. Mathematics—
Study and teaching (Elementary).   I. Title.
    QA63.O3572 2007
    372.7—dc22   2007018281

Editor: Emily Michie Birch
Production coordinator: Elizabeth Valway
Production service: Matrix Productions, Inc.
Cover design: Night & Day Design
Cover photography: Lauren Robertson
Composition: Publishers' Design and Production Services, Inc.
CD production: Nicole Russell and Marla Berry
Manufacturing: Jamie Carter

Printed in the United States of America on acid-free paper
    11   10   09   08   07   ML   1   2   3   4   5

To Brendan and Allison O'Connell
For a lifetime of happiness

On the CD-ROM

In order to be effective mathematicians, students need to develop understanding of critical math content. They need to understand number and operations, algebra, measurement, geometry, and data analysis and probability. Through continued study of these content domains, students gain a comprehensive understanding of mathematics as a subject with varied and interconnected concepts. As math teachers, we attempt to provide students with exposure to, exploration in, and reflection about the many skills and concepts that make up the study of mathematics.

Even with a deep understanding of math content, however, students may lack important skills that can assist them in their development as effective mathematicians. Along with content knowledge, students need an understanding of the processes used by mathematicians. They must learn to problem solve, communicate their ideas, reason through math situations, prove their conjectures, make connections between and among math concepts, and represent their mathematical thinking. Development of content alone does not provide students with the means to explore, express, or apply that content. As we strive to develop effective mathematicians, we are challenged to develop both students' content understanding and process skills.

The National Council of Teachers of Mathematics (2000) has outlined critical content and process standards in its *Principles and Standards for School Mathematics* document. These standards have become the roadmap for the development of textbooks, curriculum materials, and student assessments. These standards have provided a framework for thinking about what needs to be taught in math classrooms and how various skills and concepts can be blended together to create a seamless math curriculum. The first five standards outline content standards and expectations related to number and operations, algebra, geometry, measurement, and data analysis and probability. The second five standards outline the process goals of problem solving, reasoning and proof, communication, connections, and representations. A strong understanding of these standards empowers teachers to identify and select activities within their curricula to produce powerful learning. The standards provide a vision for what teachers hope their students will achieve.

This book is a part of a vital series designed to assist teachers in understanding the NCTM Process Standards and the ways in which they impact and guide student learning. An additional goal of this series is to provide practical ideas to support teachers as they ensure that the acquisition of process skills has a critical place in their math instruction. Through this series, teachers will gain an understanding of each process standard as well as gather ideas for bringing that standard to life within their math classrooms. It offers practical ideas for lesson development, implementation, and assessment that work with any curriculum. Each book in the series focuses on a critical process skill in a highlighted grade band and all books are designed to encourage reflection about teaching and learning. The series also highlights the interconnected nature of the process and content standards by showing correlations between them and showcasing activities that address multiple standards.

Students who develop an understanding of content skills and cultivate the process skills that allow them to apply that content understanding become effective mathematicians. Our goal as teachers is to support and guide students as they develop both their content knowledge and their process skills, so they are able to continue to expand and refine their understanding of mathematics. This series is a guide for math educators who aspire to teach students more than math content. It is a guide to assist teachers in understanding and teaching the critical processes through which students learn and make sense of mathematics.

Susan O'Connell
Series Editor

I am always excited to spend time in classrooms, and I want to thank the teachers and students who graciously welcomed me into their classes. It was a pleasure posing problems, hearing the student discussions, and seeing the excitement generated by the problem-solving experiences. Thanks to the following students who contributed work samples or allowed their photographs to be included in this book: Lydia Abell, Kari Adlington, Autumn Allen, Hannah Andrews, Jared Brown, Jayson Brown, Bri-anna Butler, Angelica Caruso, Robert Chaney, Tabitha Cobb, Jordan Crisler, Whitney Collins, Sam Cronk, Randall Denham, Annalie Ellis, Jacob Evans, Amane Faddoul, Elissa Foster, Keegan Girouard, David Greer, Jonathan Harris, Aaron Harten, Ben Hazel, Asianna Holmes, Dustyn Kimmett, Jordan Kingston, Aaron Lair, Jaclyn Little, Lindsay Littlejohn, Hunter McKean, Haley Nalley, Madeline Nesbit, Jake Norris, Toyin Orunja, Marcus Patterson, Joseph Ramspacher, Jeffrey Stephens, Naomi Stevens, Timothy Waters, and Eric Wickert.

And it was a pleasure collaborating with many outstanding teachers as I gathered ideas and insights for this book. Special thanks to these teachers who shared student work samples or allowed me to work side-by-side with them in their classrooms: Sarah Black, Chris Butters, Amanda Ellison, Liz Finnerty, and Katie King. A special thanks to Dr. Diana Strohecker, principal of Millersville Elementary School in Millersville, Maryland, for allowing me to work with the outstanding teachers and students in the school.

I would like to thank my colleagues in this project: Honi Bamberger, Bonnie Ennis, Brenda Hammond, Chris Oberdorf, Kelly O'Connor, Josie Robles, Karren Schultz-Ferrell, and Kim Witeck. I am thrilled to have had the opportunity to work with this outstanding group of educators.

Special thanks to Emily Birch, my Heinemann editor, for her constant attention to all of the details in this book and all of the books in this NCTM Process Standards series. Her enthusiasm for the series and her support in all aspects of its production are very much appreciated. Thanks also to Elizabeth Valway, our production coordinator, for her vision of the finished product and her insightful ways to format both the text and CD resources, and to Aaron Downey for his detailed attention to the production of this book.

Most especially, I would like to thank my family: Pat, Brendan, Katie, Allison, and Jason, for their continued support.

Problem-Solving Standard

Instructional programs from prekindergarten through grade 12 should enable all students to—

- build new mathematical knowledge through problem solving;

- solve problems that arise in mathematics and in other contexts;

- apply and adapt a variety of appropriate strategies to solve problems;

- monitor and reflect on the process of mathematical problem solving.

Reasoning and Proof Standard

Instructional programs from prekindergarten through grade 12 should enable all students to—

- recognize reasoning and proof as fundamental aspects of mathematics;

- make and investigate mathematical conjectures;

- develop and evaluate mathematical arguments and proofs;

- select and use various types of reasoning and methods of proof.

*Standards are listed with the permission of the National Council of Teachers of Mathematics (NCTM). NCTM does not endorse the content or validity of these alignments.

Communication Standard

Instructional programs from prekindergarten through grade 12 should enable all students to—

- organize and consolidate their mathematical thinking through communication;

- communicate their mathematical thinking coherently and clearly to peers, teachers, and others;

- analyze and evaluate the mathematical thinking and strategies of others;

- use the language of mathematics to express mathematical ideas precisely.

Connections Standard

Instructional programs from prekindergarten through grade 12 should enable all students to—

- recognize and use connections among mathematical ideas;

- understand how mathematical ideas interconnect and build on one another to produce a coherent whole;

- recognize and apply mathematics in contexts outside of mathematics.

Representation Standard

Instructional programs from prekindergarten through grade 12 should enable all students to—

- create and use representations to organize, record, and communicate mathematical ideas;

- select, apply, and translate among mathematical representations to solve problems;

- use representations to model and interpret physical, social, and mathematical phenomena.

NCTM Content Standards and Expectations for Grades PreK–2

NUMBER AND OPERATIONS

	Expectations
Instructional programs from prekindergarten through grade 12 should enable all students to—	**In prekindergarten through 2nd grade all students should—**
Understand numbers, ways of representing numbers, relationships among numbers, and number systems	• count with understanding and recognize "how many" in sets of objects; • use multiple models to develop initial understandings of place value and the base-ten number system; • develop understanding of the relative position and magnitude of whole numbers and of ordinal and cardinal numbers and their connections; • develop a sense of whole numbers and represent and use them in flexible ways, including relating, composing, and decomposing numbers; • connect number words and numerals to the quantities they represent, using various physical models and representations; • understand and represent commonly used fractions, such as 1/4, 1/3, and 1/2.
Understand meanings of operations and how they relate to one another	• understand various meanings of addition and subtraction of whole numbers and the relationship between the two operations; • understand the effects of adding and subtracting whole numbers; • understand situations that entail multiplication and division, such as equal groupings of objects and sharing equally.
Compute fluently and make reasonable estimates	• develop and use strategies for whole-number computations, with a focus on addition and subtraction;

	Expectations
Instructional programs from prekindergarten through grade 12 should enable all students to—	**In prekindergarten through 2nd grade all students should—**
	• develop fluency with basic number combinations for addition and subtraction; • use a variety of methods and tools to compute, including objects, mental computation, estimation, paper and pencil, and calculators.

ALGEBRA

	Expectations
Instructional programs from prekindergarten through grade 12 should enable all students to—	**In prekindergarten through 2nd grade all students should—**
Understand patterns, relations, and functions	• sort, classify, and order objects by size, number, and other properties; • recognize, describe, and extend patterns such as sequences of sounds and shapes or simple numeric patterns and translate from one representation to another; • analyze how both repeating and growing patterns are generated.
Represent and analyze mathematical situations and structures using algebraic symbols	• illustrate general principles and properties of operations, such as commutativity, using specific numbers; • use concrete, pictorial, and verbal representations to develop an understanding of invented and conventional symbolic notations.
Use mathematical models to represent and understand quantitative relationships	• model situations that involve the addition and subtraction of whole numbers, using objects, pictures, and symbols.
Analyze change in various contexts	• describe qualitative change, such as a student's growing taller; • describe quantitative change, such as a student's growing two inches in one year.

	Expectations
Instructional programs from prekindergarten through grade 12 should enable all students to—	**In prekindergarten through 2nd grade all students should—**
Analyze characteristics and properties of two- and three-dimensional geometric shapes and develop mathematical arguments about geometric relationships	• recognize, name, build, draw, compare, and sort two- and three-dimensional shapes; • describe attributes and parts of two- and three-dimensional shapes; • investigate and predict the results of putting together and taking apart two- and three-dimensional shapes.
Specify locations and describe spatial relationships using coordinate geometry and other representational systems	• describe, name, and interpret relative positions in space and apply ideas about relative position; • describe, name, and interpret direction and distance in navigating space and apply ideas about direction and distance; • find and name locations with simple relationships such as "near to" and in coordinate systems such as maps.
Apply transformations and use symmetry to analyze mathematical situations	• recognize and apply slides, flips, and turns; • recognize and create shapes that have symmetry.
Use visualization, spatial reasoning, and geometric modeling to solve problems	• create mental images of geometric shapes using spatial memory and spatial visualization; • recognize and represent shapes from different perspectives; • relate ideas in geometry to ideas in number and measurement; • recognize geometric shapes and structures in the environment and specify their location.

MEASUREMENT

	Expectations
Instructional programs from prekindergarten through grade 12 should enable all students to—	**In prekindergarten through 2nd grade all students should—**
Understand measurable attributes of objects and the units, systems, and processes of measurement	• recognize the attributes of length, volume, weight, area, and time; • compare and order objects according to these attributes; • understand how to measure using nonstandard and standard units; • select an appropriate unit and tool for the attribute being measured.
Apply appropriate techniques, tools, and formulas to determine measurements	• measure with multiple copies of units of the same size, such as paper clips laid end to end; • use repetition of a single unit to measure something larger than the unit, for instance, measuring the length of a room with a single meterstick; • use tools to measure; • develop common referents for measures to make comparisons and estimates.

DATA ANALYSIS AND PROBABILITY

	Expectations
Instructional programs from prekindergarten through grade 12 should enable all students to—	**In prekindergarten through 2nd grade all students should—**
Formulate questions that can be addressed with data and collect, organize, and display relevant data to answer them	• pose questions and gather data about themselves and their surroundings; • sort and classify objects according to their attributes and organize data about the objects; • represent data using concrete objects, pictures, and graphs.
Select and use appropriate statistical methods to analyze data	• describe parts of the data and the set of data as a whole to determine what the data show.
Develop and evaluate inferences and predictions that are based on data	• discuss events related to students' experiences as likely or unlikely.
Understand and apply basic concepts of probability	

Introduction to Problem Solving
Grades PreK–2

The Problem-Solving Standard

Solving problems is not only a goal of learning mathematics but also a major means of doing so.

—National Council of Teachers of Mathematics,
Principles and Standards for School Mathematics

Why Focus on Problem Solving?

Traditionally, problem solving was viewed as a distinct topic, introduced to students after they had mastered basic skills. In today's classrooms, however, problem solving is recognized as the central focus of mathematics instruction. The ability to solve problems is the ultimate goal of mathematics. It is why we teach students to add, subtract, multiply, and divide. It is why we teach them to work with fractions, measurement, and geometry. Our goal is not for students to perform isolated computations, but rather to be able to apply their varied math skills to solve problems. But problem solving is more than just a goal of learning mathematics, it is also a critical process, woven across the entire mathematics curriculum, through which students are able to explore and understand mathematics (NCTM 2000, 52). Through problem-solving experiences, students learn to challenge their thinking about data and probability, test their ideas about numbers and operations, apply their skills in geometry and measurement, and evaluate their understandings of algebra. Through problem-solving tasks, students develop an understanding of math content and ultimately use that content understanding to find solutions to problems. Problem solving is both the process by which students explore mathematics and the goal of learning mathematics.

One objective of problem-solving instruction is to enable students to use their repertoire of math skills to solve problems. But it takes more than isolated math skills

1

to be an effective problem solver. It also takes a variety of thinking skills that allow students to organize ideas, select appropriate strategies, and determine the reasonableness of solutions. It takes an understanding of how to use and adapt strategies to fit the problem situation. And it takes an ability to reflect on how we solve problems to help us better understand our own thought processes and identify why we select and apply various strategies.

In the past, problem solving may have been viewed as an isolated assignment (e.g., a list of word problems), but today problem solving has an integrated role in the math classroom. Teachers begin lessons by posing a problem, then skills and strategies are developed throughout the lesson as the problem is explored, and those newly acquired skills allow students to successfully find a solution. Problem solving becomes both the starting point and the ending point to well-balanced mathematics lessons. Developing students' computational skills is important, but teaching those skills in a problem-solving context ensures that students not only understand the skill but see the meaningfulness of learning the skill and understand how to apply it to real-world situations. "Problem solving is the process by which students experience the power and usefulness of mathematics in the world around them" (NCTM 1989, 75).

What Is the Problem-Solving Process Standard?

The National Council of Teachers of Mathematics (NCTM) has developed standards to support and guide teachers as they develop classroom lessons and create activities to build their students' mathematical understandings. Some of those standards delineate the content to be addressed in the math classroom, while other standards address the processes by which students explore and use mathematics. Problem solving is a critical math process, and the components of the NCTM Problem Solving Process Standard reflect its complex nature. Instructional programs (NCTM 2000, 52) should enable students to:

- build new mathematical knowledge through problem solving;

- solve problems that arise in mathematics and in other contexts;

- apply and adapt a variety of appropriate strategies to solve problems;

- monitor and reflect on the process of mathematical problem solving.

Throughout this book, we explore ways to assist primary students in building new math knowledge through problem-solving tasks. Highlighted problem-solving activities may be presented in math contexts as well as real-world contexts. We explore, in depth, the various problem-solving strategies that support young students in finding solutions, and we identify techniques for helping our students reflect and monitor their problem solving. We will dive into the NCTM process standard of problem solving in order to better understand it and find ways to bring it to life within our primary classrooms.

Creating Effective Problem Solvers

In my early experiences with teaching problem solving, I began much as my own teachers had: I assigned problems to students and expected them to be able to solve the problems on their own. I quickly recognized my students' anxiety and frustration. I soon learned that assigning problems and then correcting those problems did not create successful problem solvers. I began to break down the skills needed to solve problems and find opportunities to guide my students in developing some specific strategies to help them organize their thinking. Through a combination of modeling, providing opportunities for exploration, facilitating discussions about thinking, and prompting students to reflect on their experiences, I observed the continually increasing efficiency with which my students solved problems. The more they explored and analyzed problem-solving strategies, the more successful they became. Surprisingly, not just the most capable of my students showed progress, but all of them did. As I demonstrated various strategies to attack problems and began to let my students see math problems through visual and hands-on demonstrations, their skills improved. And my skills improved, too! The more comfortable I became at teaching problem solving, the more confident I became about my ability to help my students understand a process that had once seemed so complicated and abstract.

With an understanding of the problem-solving process and a repertoire of strategies to assist our students in dealing with problem situations, our anxiety and frustration lessens and our enthusiasm and confidence grow. Not all students can become effective problem solvers on their own, but with the help of a confident and capable teacher, all students can significantly improve their problem-solving abilities.

Developing Skills and Attitudes

Developing the problem-solving abilities of primary students is a challenging and complex task. It requires attention to the building of mathematical skills and thinking processes as well as attention to the development of positive attitudes toward problem solving. Both skills and attitudes must be strengthened to produce truly effective problem solvers.

Problem solving is a process that requires students to follow a series of steps to find a solution. Although some students may intuitively follow a process, many students need to be taught how to proceed to reach a solution. Another important goal in teaching students to solve problems is assisting them in developing strategies or plans for solving problems. Although choosing a mathematical operation (e.g., addition or subtraction) is frequently the way to solve a problem, alternate strategies are often needed. Helping students learn strategies such as drawing pictures, finding patterns, making tables, making lists, guessing and checking, working backward, or using logical reasoning gives students a wide variety of strategies to employ during problem solving. Problem solving requires this knowledge of strategies as well as the ability to determine when each strategy would be best used. The more our students practice these strategies, the more confident they become in their ability to solve problems and apply mathematics in meaningful ways.

The development of a positive attitude toward problem solving is crucial to student success. As teachers, we are instrumental in helping our students develop the attitudes needed to become successful problem solvers. Positive attitudes are built on an awareness of the nature of problem solving:

■ *Problem solving requires patience.* It is not always possible to find a quick answer, and quick answers are often incorrect. Problem solving is not judged on speed but on the reasonableness of the final solution.

■ *Problem solving requires persistence.* Students may need to try several strategies before finding one that will work. Students must have confidence that they can find a solution, even if it is not immediately apparent.

■ *Problem solving requires risk taking.* Students need to be willing to try their "hunches," hoping that they may lead to a solution. Students must feel comfortable making mistakes, as problem solving is a process filled with mistakes that often lead to solutions.

■ *Problem solving requires cooperation.* Students must often be willing to share ideas, build on one another's thoughts, and work together to find a solution.

Students become successful problem solvers when they are instructed in a climate that rewards patience, persistence, risk taking, and cooperation. As teachers, we have a critical role in establishing a positive climate for problem-solving instruction.

How This Book Will Help You

This book is designed to help you better understand the NCTM problem-solving standard. It explores problem solving as both a process through which students learn mathematics and a skill that enables them to apply the mathematics they have learned. The mathematical goals of students in prekindergarten through grade 2 are specifically addressed, and practical ideas are provided for helping primary students become effective problem solvers.

This book presents ideas for developing a problem-centered approach to teaching mathematics within your classroom. We will see how problem solving can set a context for learning math skills, can excite and engage students, and can help students discover insights and better understand math ideas. We explore ways in which problem solving enriches our math classrooms and nurtures enthusiasm, curiosity, and insight.

Within this book you will find a variety of ideas to help you better understand the problem-solving process, as well as specific strategies including Choose an Operation; Find a Pattern; Make a Table; Make an Organized List; Draw a Picture or Diagram; Guess, Check, and Revise; Use Logical Reasoning; and Work Backward. These strategies help students organize their thinking, figure out ways to approach and simplify problems, and ultimately find their way to solutions. We explore practical ways to support our students as they develop these thinking skills, knowing that the groundwork for each strategy is laid in the primary grades. As we investigate a variety of problem-solving strategies, we delve into their underlying skills in order to unearth the complexity and importance of each strategy. A variety of activities appropriate for primary students are shared for each strategy. Specific grade levels are not indicated on each activity, as problem-solving skills do not develop by grade level, but rather depend on students' prior knowledge and previous exposure to each strategy. Some primary students enter school intuitively demonstrating a strategy, while others may need exposure and repeated practice to develop the same thinking skill. Teacher tips are shared highlighting important points to emphasize when working with students. Examples of student work are presented for each strategy, including samples of students' communication about their problem solving. The student work samples offer a glimpse into students' thinking as their skills develop.

Once we have explored the problem-solving standard in depth, you will see how it connects to the math content standards in Chapter 13, titled *Problem Solving Across the Content Standards*. Through sample classroom activities, we explore the interconnectedness of the content and process standards. We discuss sample problem-solving tasks that blend with the math content taught in grades prekindergarten through 2 in numbers and operations, algebra, geometry, measurement, and data and probability. Student work is shared to illustrate these lessons, and you will be asked to reflect on the combined teaching of math content and the problem-solving process.

In this book we also discuss the assessment of problem solving, including the use of observations, interviews, and rubrics to assess students' skills. While this book is designed to help you better understand the NCTM Problem-Solving Standard and to provide you with practical ideas and classroom activities related to the standard, it is also intended to stimulate thought about teaching and learning. Following each chapter, several questions prompt you to reflect on the content of the chapter whether alone or with a group of your colleagues. Taking a moment to reflect on the ideas presented and to relate them to your teaching experiences and observations of your students will help you better process the ideas and apply them to your students' specific needs.

A very important component of this book is the inclusion of the practical resources needed to implement the ideas explored throughout the chapters. The accompanying CD is filled with a variety of teacher-ready materials to help you implement a problem-solving program in your school or classroom. Graphic organizers, evaluation forms, a scoring rubric, and icons are all available, as well as a variety of practice problems for your students. The practice problems range from simple to complex. Some of the CD activities appear as teacher notes, providing you with directions for conducting the activities in your classroom. Other activities are provided in worksheet format for those students who may be able to work independently. If your students are unable to independently read the directions, however, these activities can be modified through teacher-read directions or simply be used to generate ideas for similar problem-solving activities or classroom demonstration. Select those activities that suit your students' level of expertise, and continue to challenge your students with more sophisticated problem-solving tasks as their skills improve. And the activities and resources on the

CD can be easily modified to suit your students' specific needs. Change the data to make an activity less or more challenging, or insert familiar names and places to engage and motivate your students.

It is hoped that this book will enhance your understanding of the problem-solving standard and provide you with insights, resources, and practical ideas to develop your students' problem-solving skills. When we, as teachers, better understand the complexity and importance of problem solving, we are better able to identify, select, and design meaningful tasks for our students. It is hoped that the varied instructional practices highlighted in this book will assist you in developing your students' skills and expanding your own understandings. Most certainly, as we reflect on and develop our teaching skills, our students' problem-solving skills will increase as well.

Questions for Discussion

1. Were you taught how to solve math problems or just assigned problems to solve? How did you feel about math problem solving when you were a student in the math classroom? In what ways do your past experiences and attitudes about problem solving influence your teaching of problem solving?

2. If students show competence with computational skills but lack problem-solving skills, how might it affect their math achievement? What possible problems might they experience?

3. What attitudes are essential to be an effective problem solver? How might you support students in developing these attitudes?

4. What skills are essential to be an effective problem solver? How might you help your students to acquire those skills?

Building Math Understanding Through Problem Solving

A problem-based approach to teaching mathematics uses interesting and well-selected problems to launch mathematical lessons and engage students. In this way, new ideas, techniques, and mathematical relationships emerge and become the focus of discussion.

—National Council of Teachers of Mathematics,
Principles and Standards for School Mathematics

Primary students come to school excited about learning. They enjoy discovering new ideas and solving real problems. Even at very young ages, our students are capable of mathematical thinking and problem solving. When we pose meaningful problems and allow students to explore those problems, we create an environment in which students strengthen both their math content skills and their problem-solving skills.

We strive to provide a strong math foundation for our primary students. We want them to be able to use their math knowledge to solve problems rather than simply memorize facts and mechanically perform computations. Problem solving is both a goal and a vehicle for our students. Our goal is for them to use their understanding of math concepts and skills to find solutions to the problems we pose, and the problem-solving experiences are the vehicle through which our students explore, discuss, and develop a variety of math skills. We want our students to learn *about* problem solving as well as learn *through* problem solving.

While traditional math teaching was teacher-directed and skills-based, recent research and professional discussions support the power of problem-based instruction (Hiebert et al., 1997; Lester and Charles, 2003; Trafton and Thiessen, 1999; Van de Walle and Lovin, 2005). We recognize its value in helping students better understand important math ideas. Through problem-based experiences, students are able to explore math content as they solve problems. Problem-based instruction is a significant tool for helping students examine, predict, observe, discover, and ultimately use mathematics.

Teaching Math Through Problems

Most of us were told how to do math. Our teachers identified key ideas and told us what we needed to know, and then asked us to practice and memorize specific skills and procedures. Students with strong rote memory skills were able to effectively memorize facts and procedures, often realizing later that they did not understand what they had memorized. Students with poor rote skills struggled with memorizing ideas that had no meaning to them and often became frustrated with mathematics. Problem-solving tasks provide our students with opportunities to explore and understand the concepts and processes that we were asked to simply memorize.

In recent years we have recognized that problem-solving tasks motivate and engage students in a way that lecture and drill-and-practice tasks are unable to do. Students are naturally inquisitive. They like to explore, investigate, and hypothesize. They become excited and energized by new problems.

In problem-based instruction, rather than telling students key math ideas, problems are posed to engage students in exploration and promote thinking about the important mathematical concepts. Students explore problems with partners or groups and are guided in that exploration by the teacher. Students are actively engaged in learning. They are asked to communicate their ideas, share their insights, apply their previously learned knowledge to new situations, reflect on their experiences, and ultimately discover new math ideas. Through problem tasks, new knowledge is built on existing knowledge. In problem-based instruction, the process of learning is as important as the content being learned. Students are learning new ideas but are also learning "how" to learn new ideas.

A Look at Problem-Based Instruction

In problem-based instruction, problems are posed that become a starting point for student learning. The problem investigation sets the context through which students are challenged to use their current skills to develop new understandings. As students look at a math concept or skill in a problem context, they ask questions, test ideas, and ultimately grow to better understand the concept. We are often surprised at the complexity of problems that can be solved by primary students even before they "learn" the math concepts.

The teacher posed the following problem to her kindergarten students:

> **I have one sticker for each student in the class. I have 10 red stickers. The rest of my stickers are blue. How many blue stickers do I have?**

The kindergarten students explored the sticker problem with partners. While they were unable to use a subtraction algorithm to get the answer, one pair of students drew a sticker for each person in the class and then colored 10 of them red. Then they colored the rest of their stickers blue and counted the blue stickers to find their answer. Another pair of students placed 10 red counters on their desk and then added blue counters until they got to 17 (the number of students in their class). In both cases, the students used their understanding of the problem situation to find a means for representing and solving the problem, and in both cases, their methods laid a foundation for understanding the operations of addition and subtraction.

A first-grade teacher posed the following problem to her class:

There are 5 bags of apples on the table and there are 5 apples in each bag. How many apples are on the table?

Students solved the problem in a variety of ways. Some drew the bags and apples (or circles to represent the apples) and then counted each individual apple, while others used their understanding of skip-counting to count by bags (5, 10, 15, 20, 25). Still others added (5 + 5 + 5 + 5 + 5) to find the answer. Though these students did not understand the use of multiplication to solve the problem, their varied approaches show critical understanding (i.e., skip-counting and repeated addition) that will support them as they learn to use multiplication as a faster, more efficient way to solve similar problems.

A second-grade teacher posed the following problem to his students:

We have 40 cookies for our class party. We want to share them so that everyone gets the same number of cookies. How many cookies can each student have?

When exploring the cookie problem, a traditional division problem, Jill and Marty drew 20 circles to represent the children in the class and began putting one block (representing a cookie) in each circle, then going back and putting a second block in each circle, until all of the cookies had been evenly distributed (see Figure 1–1). Drew and Timmy drew pictures of the 20 students and drew circles next to each student to represent the cookies they could eat. Before understanding the traditional algorithm for division, these students were able to understand the concept of fair sharing and were able to find the correct solution. Through their own investigations, discussions, and insights, they gained experience with the math concept. Now, even before it appears in their textbook, they have begun to discover the concept of division and it makes sense to them!

During problem explorations, not all students may find the correct solution. Not all students will do it in a way we expect. To solve the cookie problem, Alex and Hannah also drew circles for each student, but began by putting several cookies in each circle and then ran out of cookies, leaving some circles, or students, without any cookies. Some students seem to intuitively find methods for solving problems, while others struggle with determining the problem, deciding on a strategy, or finding a reasonable solution. Class problem-solving experiences and attention to the development of problem-solving skills (see later chapters) help all students become more effective problem solvers. The teacher's role is to guide and refine students' understanding. The

Figure 1–1 *Active engagement in problem-solving experiences helps students make sense of math.*

way explorations are set up (i.e., the directions for the task, the availability of materials, the selection of partners), the questions that are asked (e.g., "Should every student get the same amount of cookies?"), and the way sharing is facilitated following the problem-solving task (i.e., class discussions or circle time to share approaches and solutions) support students in the development of their skills. And following problem tasks, teachers use the insights that have been gained to design lessons to further students' math understanding.

Elements of Problem-Based Instruction

Problem-based instruction is more than simply posing a problem and asking students to solve it. In problem-based instruction, teachers are challenged to support students as they solve problems. They must select appropriate tasks, guide students as they engage in the tasks, facilitate discussions and sharing about solutions, and assess students' understanding of the math content and problem-solving process. Teachers' observations during the problem-solving tasks often result in ideas for related classroom lessons or mini-workshops. These essential teacher responsibilities influence the success of the problem-solving activity.

Selecting tasks that lead students to important math learning is fundamental. Good problems set the stage for our students to explore and discover significant math ideas. If selected carefully, problem-solving tasks can motivate and engage students in learning math, can illustrate the application of math skills, can support students in the development of new math understanding, and can provide assessment of students' strengths and weaknesses. Meaningful tasks do not need to be lengthy and can be set in a math context or a real-world context, but they need to address important math skills and promote thought about those skills. A look at content standards and indicators will provide you with ideas of critical skills.

Since mathematics is about both content and process, problem-solving activities can lead students to insights about either. First graders were asked how many people could sit at 6 square tables if one person could sit at each side of a table. Students explored number concepts as they drew and counted tables, skip-counted, or added to find their answers. They explored math processes as they worked together to decide on the question, figured out how to display the data (e.g., a model, picture, or table), observed the data for patterns in the numbers (e.g., 4, 8, 12, 16 . . .), and shared solutions and methods. Through the selection of appropriate problems, students can be challenged to develop and refine their thinking about math content and processes.

CLASSROOM-TESTED TIP

Preparing for the Problem-Solving Task

Consider the following questions as you introduce students to the problem:
   Do students understand the context for the problem?

■ Will you need to have a brief discussion about zoos or amusement parks in order for students to understand the task?

Do students have available materials and adequate work space?

■ Will your students be more successful if they have hands-on materials available?

■ Will they need paper, pencils, crayons, glue?

■ Is there enough space for them to work?

What pairings or groupings will work best for the task?

■ Will students be more successful with a partner or will groups of 3 or 4 work well for this task?

■ Are there students who do not work well together or others who would benefit from each other's help?

Will students be asked to produce written work? If so, what is expected?

■ Are you asking students to draw pictures or write to show their work?

■ Are you asking them to create a product (e.g., a plan for how to share cookies or arrange tables for a party)?

Do you anticipate that any students will need extra support?

■ Are there groups that you should observe more frequently than others or groups that you might like to join?

■ Are there any groups that might need a modification of the problem to make it simpler or more challenging?

The Role of Communication

Guiding students as they explore problems is critical to the success of the problem-solving experience. Support comes in many shapes and sizes. As we observe students during problem tasks, we look for cues to let us know when support or encouragement may be needed or when additional challenges are appropriate. Through questioning to guide our students' thinking or stimulate their ideas, or through class debriefing to highlight discoveries, teachers play an active role in ensuring that students are thinking as they work and are learning from the experience.

When we observe students solving problems, we often notice students who are intuitively able to apply strategies as they work through a problem. Others, however, appear to be perplexed as to how to approach the problem and experience great difficulty with the task. During problem-solving tasks, we are challenged to help some of our students recognize what they may have intuitively done to solve the problem, and support others in discovering insights from those around them who may be using appropriate strategies. Language in the math classroom is a key for helping students recognize their own and each other's thinking. It makes thinking visible within the classroom.

Through teacher talk, we introduce the task, clarify the question, and guide students in the investigation. After posing the problem, we might clarify it using some examples to help students understand their task. As students work together to solve problems, we ask questions to stimulate thought or redirect efforts. Our words are influential in helping students discover ideas.

Student talk is also a critical component of problem-based instruction. Students should work with partners or groups to foster math talk about their thinking. Through partner and group work we allow students to struggle with ideas and build on each other's insights or allow a natural form of tutoring to occur as some students explain their insights to others.

Through facilitating class discussions we allow students to express their thoughts and insights and allow others to hear their ideas and meld them into their own. Through presentations and written products (e.g., drawings or writing) to share their solutions and approaches, we provide opportunities for all students to see multiple solutions and approaches as well as to hear related ideas as they work to support their own findings.

In problem-based instruction, the goal is not a correct answer, although we do love correct answers! The goal is to explore a task, determine a strategy to get to a solution, and learn about math along the way. Students might find varied, but equally reasonable, ways to get to a solution. Allowing students to report about their insights and share their strategies is important in extending the understanding of all students within the classroom. Even wrong answers or illogical strategies are part of the learning process, as errors often lead to insights for our students. And listening to students' errors provides us with valuable insight into their thinking.

Problems as a Teaching Tool

As we become more comfortable allowing students to explore problems even before some skills have been taught, we begin to recognize that students often discover many math ideas on their own. Posing problems frequently enough to allow students to explore skills, learn to apply skills, and in so doing advance their thinking, arouse their curiosity, and generate insights, is a goal of problem-based instruction. Problems are a tool for extending our students' understanding of math.

Problem solving is both a process and a skill. It is a process, a way in which students learn about math ideas. Through problem explorations, students expand their understanding of math concepts and develop their math skills. But problem solving is also a skill to be learned by students. Through the development of some critical problem-solving strategies, which we explore in the following chapters, students can become more skillful at solving even complex math problems.

Questions for Discussion

1. How is the teacher's role in problem-based instruction different from his or her role in the traditional drill-and-practice style of teaching math? How is the student's role different?

2. What is the role of teacher questioning during problem tasks? What is the role of student-to-student talk?

3. How will problem-based tasks provide teachers with insight and guidance for the development of future lessons?

4. What can the teacher do to support students who are having difficulty solving problems?

2

Guiding Students Through the Problem-Solving Process

The instructional goal is that students will build an increasing repertoire of strategies, approaches, and familiar problems; it is the problem-solving process that is most important, not just the answer.

—National Council of Teachers of Mathematics,
Curriculum and Evaluation Standards for School Mathematics

Teaching math concepts through a problem-based approach provides opportunities for our students to discover and refine important math ideas. While some students may intuitively know how to approach the problem tasks, organize their thinking, and select appropriate strategies to find solutions, many others need opportunities to identify and develop their problem-solving skills. Whether we are helping our intuitive problem solvers refine their skills or helping our struggling problem solvers develop their skills, attention to the problem-solving process and key problem-solving strategies is essential.

The Problem-Solving Process

Problem solving is a multistep task. Successful problem solvers move through a series of steps toward the solution. This does not mean that every student thinks through each step in the same way, but that a process occurs within the heads of problem solvers to help them move through a problem from start to finish. Polya (2004) first identified steps in the problem-solving process, and those steps have been used, discussed, and adapted in numerous problem-solving programs and curricula. Helping students identify this process helps them see problem solving as a series of steps that will lead them to the eventual solution. Focusing primary students on each step of the problem-solving process allows them to identify a place to begin and then reveals reasonable steps to move them closer to the answer, making problem solving doable. It helps our students identify the problem and important data that they will need to solve the problem. It alerts them to possible ways to find solutions, and offers a reminder to check their thinking. Essentially, the problem-solving process helps our students see what goes on in the mind of a good problem solver.

Following is a checklist that guides students through the critical steps of the problem-solving process:

Problem-Solving Checklist

Understand the question.
Choose a plan.
Try your plan.
Check your answer.
Reflect on what you've done.

Problem-Solving Notes

UNDERSTAND - Write the problem in your own words.

PLAN - How will you solve the problem?

TRY - Show your work.

CHECK
Did you check your work?   Yes   No

Does your answer make sense?   Yes   No

REFLECT - Tell how you solved the problem.

May be copied for classroom use. © 2007 by Susan O'Connell from *Introduction to Problem Solving: Grades PreK–2* (Portsmouth, NH: Heinemann).

Figure 2–1 *Asking students to record their ideas, or having the teacher record class ideas, helps them recognize and remember the steps of the problem-solving process.*

Breaking Down the Process

Step 1: Understand the Question

This first step in the problem-solving process asks students to think about the problem and decide what they are being asked to solve. This is an important step in focusing students for the problem-solving task ahead. We have all experienced watching students labor over finding the answer to the *wrong question*. If students are uncertain what they are being asked to solve, it is unlikely that they will be able to arrive at a reasonable solution.

In this initial step in the problem-solving process, students are asked to restate the problem in their own words. Ask them to identify the question—to tell you what they are being asked to solve or find out. Students might be given written problems and asked to identify the question, either by circling the "question" part of the problem or by writing the question in their own words. Consider having students work in pairs or groups to determine what the problem is asking them to do. Hearing each other's thoughts will strengthen their ability to identify the question. And understanding the question leads our students to discussions about the data they believe will be useful in solving the problem.

When practicing this first step in the problem-solving process, students do not need to solve each problem that is posed. Isolating the skill of identifying and understanding the question and practicing that skill without moving through all of the steps of the problem-solving process helps students strengthen their skills in this area.

Step 2: Choose a Plan

In this critical step, students must decide *how* to solve the problem. Students will need to identify a plan or strategy for solving the problem. Students may recognize that the problem can be solved with one of the basic operations (e.g., addition or subtraction) or they may discover that an alternate strategy—making a list, a table, or diagram; working backward; finding a pattern; guessing and checking; or using logical reasoning—may be more effective for solving the problem. Students will need to identify the known data (the data that appear in the problem) that will help them solve the problem and will have to determine what to do with that data to get to the solution. Students may look for key concepts to help them decide on a strategy (see Chapter 4) or may relate the problem to other familiar problems in order to help them decide how to proceed. There is often more than one way to solve a problem. Primary students will need to be introduced to a variety of problem-solving strategies and then helped to figure out when each strategy might be appropriate to help them find a solution. Discussions at this stage will help students appreciate the different ways that problems can be solved. And whenever possible, having students predict the answer, after they have determined their plan, will provide them with a benchmark later in the process as they look back to check the reasonableness of their answer.

Step 3: Try Your Plan

Now it's time for students to put the selected strategy to use. In this step, the student uses his or her strategy to attempt to find a solution. At times, students may try their plans and find that those plans do not lead to a solution. This is an important realization. Students need to recognize that trying and then eliminating a strategy is okay. Finding a solution does not always happen on the first try. Recognizing that a strategy was unsuccessful and deciding on an alternate strategy are important skills in building effective problem solvers.

Step 4: Check Your Answer

Traditionally, this step has focused on checking for calculation errors. While checking for arithmetic accuracy is important, it is equally important that students recognize that checking their answers includes checking the reasonableness of the answers. If students predicted an answer before trying their plans, this is the time for them to compare their predicted and actual answers to see if they are compatible. Encourage students to ask themselves questions such as "Does this answer make sense?" or "Is something not quite right here?"

Even without a prediction, students are often able to recognize when an answer does not seem reasonable. Asking students to write a summary statement that relates their answer to the question will force them to look at the question and answer together and may help them recognize unreasonable answers. For young students, consider providing them with a slotted sentence for their answer: "Jerry had __ peanuts in his 6 bags.". Rather than simply writing the number, students have an opportunity to see the number in context and may recognize answers that don't make sense. This technique is especially helpful for those students who rush from problem to problem, doing the calculations and never looking back to check for reasonableness.

Consider the following problem:

There were 75 students on the playground. 30 students were boys. How many girls were on the playground?

Summary: 75 students were on the playground. 30 were boys and 105 were girls.

The realization: *"That can't be right! There were only 75 students on the playground!"*

Step 5: Reflect on What You've Done

Once the problem has been solved, it is time for students to sit back and reflect on their actions and insights throughout the process. Students might be asked to explain how they solved the problem or to tell why they think their answer is correct. They might be asked to share other ways of solving the problem or to reflect on what was easy or hard about the task. This step allows students to process what they've done, and it gives teachers valuable insight into students' thinking. In the teaching of problem solving, this is a critical step as it supports students in better understanding their own thinking (metacognition). It is the step in which students recognize and verbalize how they solved a problem and why they solved it in that way.

CLASSROOM-TESTED TIP

Estimating the Answer

Once students have decided on their plan for solving a problem, it is a good time for them to stop and think about what the predicted answer might be. When students are able to predict or estimate the answer, they are better able to judge the reasonableness of the answer when they calculate it later in the process. Many errors occur when students make calculation mistakes and have not previously considered what the answer might be. Seeing a discrepancy between his or her predicted answer and a calculated answer sends up a red flag, alerting the student to take a second look at the answer.

There may be times when predicting an answer is difficult. While students may be able to do some mental math to estimate that the sum of 13 and 5 will be about 20, they may have trouble predicting answers to other problems, such as those for which a diagram might be needed to find a solution. Predicting is a step that can help students later in the problem-solving process when they are checking to see if their answer is reasonable. If they are unable to do it, it's okay. Teach students to move on and continue with the remaining steps in the problem-solving process.

Recording Steps in Solving Problems

Showing students how to use writing as a tool to organize and record their ideas will help them proceed through, and remember, the steps to solving problems. Many teachers use checklists or worksheets to help students internalize the thinking process. Initially, using a checklist helps students understand each step of the process. They are able to see the steps modeled and they benefit from moving through each step until it becomes routine. In the early stages, teachers might simply talk about each step and record ideas on a chart for students to see. Later, students might be asked to do their own writing on a process checklist or worksheet like the examples on the CD. These checklists or worksheets help students organize their thinking and remind them of the steps in the problem-solving process. They support students by allowing them to process their ideas as they record them. Teachers might use different formats for student writing, as illustrated in the varied formats on the CD, but the main components (the steps in the problem-solving process) remain consistent to help students remember important steps to consider when solving problems. Some teachers prefer worksheets on which students record their ideas in each section as they move through each step of the process. Others may prefer to offer students open-ended prompts to guide them through the steps, as in the following examples:

Understand the Question	I (We) need to find out . . .
	I (We) already know . . .
Choose a Plan	To get the answer I (we) could . . .
	I (We) think the answer will be . . .
Try Your Plan	Here is my (our) work . . .
Check Your Answer	My (Our) answer makes sense because . . .
Reflect on What You've Done.	I (We) got my (our) answer by . . .
	I (We) had trouble . . . . but I (we) . . .

Many students are familiar with K-W-L charts (What I *Know*, What I *Want* to Know, What I *Learned*) from using them to record ideas in other (nonmath) content areas. Using modified K-W-L charts, like the ones on the CD, can be an effective way for students to record their ideas as they work through the problem-solving process. Regardless of which format you choose, these recording tools support your students as they explore the thinking process required when solving math problems.

As students become more skilled at the process, a written checklist or worksheet may no longer be needed and may even become frustrating to some students who have internalized the problem-solving process and are now focusing their attentions on other problem-solving skills. Stopping at each step to record their actions may begin to distract them from solving the problem. Our knowledge of our students' abilities, gathered through constant monitoring and assessment, helps us recognize those students who will benefit from a step-by-step approach and those who will be more effective without the structured checklist.

Providing a checklist for selected students is a good way to address the different needs of the students in our classrooms. Students can be asked to make notes on the checklist as they proceed through the steps of the process, or the checklist can be used to stimulate discussion among partners, teams, or the entire class. The checklist might be posted in the classroom to support students during class discussions or as a resource to which they can refer during independent work. It serves to remind students of the important steps in the problem-solving process.

Helping Students Get "Unstuck"

Students can become stuck when attempting to solve math problems. When solutions are not immediately apparent, students can become frustrated and give up. Helping them learn ways to get themselves "unstuck" is an important lesson in their growth as problem solvers.

As students become stuck during classroom problem-solving experiences, we guide them with suggestions and encouragement. It is important, however, that after they have successfully solved the problem, students are asked to reflect on how they got "unstuck." Asking students to talk about what they did to get back on track will help them recognize ways to keep moving forward in the problem-solving process and will benefit all students in the class as they share experiences and begin to develop a repertoire of strategies for dealing with those frustrating moments.

Following are some self-help strategies for getting "unstuck." You might develop a class list of strategies based on your students' experiences. Similar ideas can be shared with parents during a parent night at school, as shown on the CD, providing them with ideas on how to guide their children through home problem-solving activities.

- **Restate the problem in your own words.**

  Do you understand what you are being asked to solve? Restate the problem in your own words. You need to understand the problem before you can solve it.

- **Jot down ideas.**

  Jot down a plan for how to solve the problem. You might list the important information or draw a diagram of the problem to get you started.

- **Use a manipulative.**

  Use everyday objects (paper clips, toothpicks, pennies) to represent the items in the problem. Act out the problem with the manipulatives.

- **Talk about the problem.**

  Talk out loud to yourself or to someone else. Talk about the problem and what you think you should do.

- **Think of a similar problem.**

  Does this problem remind you of another problem that you have solved? How did you solve that one? Try that strategy. Does it work here?

- **Cross out unnecessary information.**

  Is the problem confusing? Does it have too much information? Reread the problem and cross out any information that isn't needed to solve the problem.

- **Try a different strategy.**

  If what you're doing doesn't seem to be working, try something else. Is there a different strategy that you think might work? Try it and see.

- **Take a break.**

  Are you getting frustrated? Take a break for a few minutes. Think about or do something else. Then return to the problem refreshed and ready to begin again.

- **Give yourself a pep talk.**

  Think of a problem you solved by sticking with it. Remember a time when you were frustrated but kept on trying until you found the answer. Remind yourself that you can do it!

Involving Students in Instruction

Teaching problem solving is teaching students to think in an organized manner. It is the process of helping students recognize how logical and productive thinking works. To make thinking visible to our students, we can use techniques such as think-alouds, cooperative learning activities, visual demonstrations, and hands-on experiences. By transforming thinking from an abstract idea to a visible activity, we keep students engaged in the lessons, strengthen their understanding, and help them gain the skills they need to become more organized thinkers.

It is important that we model our thinking by speaking aloud to students as we proceed through demonstration problems together. This think-aloud process helps us clearly show our students what goes on in our heads as we think through problem situations. By sharing examples of logical thinking and by modeling thoughtful questions and reasonable conclusions, we highlight for students what should be happening in their own heads during the problem-solving process.

In addition, it is important that students have opportunities to discuss strategies with one another as they formulate and test ideas about how to proceed with each problem. Cooperative-learning strategies are valuable tools during problem-solving instruction, as they allow students to hear each other's thoughts and help each child expand his or her repertoire of ideas. Working with partners or groups gives students the opportunity to test their ideas on others or analyze their teammates' ideas and solutions. Group work helps students monitor their thinking, analyze their progress, and discuss alternate methods of solving each problem. Working with others also helps reduce the anxiety that often comes with "standing alone" and allows students to take risks and gain confidence in their own abilities. It allows them to practice their thinking in a safe and comfortable environment.

Visual and hands-on demonstrations are also critical in helping students understand problem-solving strategies. We might use an overhead projector, video visualizer, blackboard, or white board to demonstrate strategies. Using hands-on materials to simulate a problem or create a diagram helps our students see ways to re-create what is happening in the problem. As students develop a deeper understanding of the strategy, the visual and hands-on examples will naturally give way to more abstract thinking.

Students need repeated practice with problem-solving strategies, and they need to be given opportunities to decide which strategies apply to which problems. After initial exposure to each strategy (e.g., finding patterns, making tables, or drawing pictures), the teacher should give students opportunities to look at a mixed group of problems and determine which strategy makes sense in each situation. Students will often remember certain problems that were done in hands-on or visual ways and connect the new problems to these old, familiar problems. As students realize, "That's just like the pizza problem!" they will begin to recognize that applying the same strategy ("We drew a picture of the pizzas") may be the way to approach this problem, too. During these types of activities, our students need opportunities to hear each other's ideas as they discuss the use of different strategies, because often more than one strategy may be effective. In the following chapters, we explore the development of problem-solving strategies in greater detail.

Finally, connecting problem-solving instruction to students' lives helps them see the purpose for learning each strategy. Throughout this book, you will see an emphasis on using real-world problems during problem-solving instruction. During early instruction, problems should reflect the interests of young students and may deal with games, pets, holidays, or food. Posing problems in real-world contexts makes problem solving fun and engaging.

CLASSROOM-TESTED TIP

Modeling Your Thinking

The think-aloud is a valuable tool when teaching problem solving. During a think-aloud, the teacher says aloud what she is thinking while working through the problem. The teacher verbalizes more than the math content; she also verbalizes when she is confused and what she does as a result of the confusion, or verbalizes her insights and discoveries as she observes math data. In a think-aloud, students are able to hear the teacher's thoughts as she analyzes the situation and makes decisions:

> *"Let's see—I know that Andrew's train had 12 cars and Kevin's train had 18 cars. I need to know how much longer Kevin's train was. It's like when we lined them up next to each other—we're comparing them. That's what we do when we subtract! I'll just subtract 18 – 12."*
>
> *"I predicted that the answer would be 25, but I got 45. Something is not right. It wouldn't make sense for the answer to be 45. I think I'll go back and check to see if I made a mistake."*

Teachers who are cognizant of common errors can direct their think-alouds to those mistakes.

A Word About Word Problems

When we think of problem solving, most of us think about traditional word problems. Word problems of the past were written in a very predictable format (i.e., There were 12 girls and 14 boys in the class. How many students were in the class altogether?). These tasks were termed *word problems* to distinguish them from routine computational tasks. Word problems often appeared at the end of the page in our textbooks or at the end of a chapter. The solution strategies were also generally predictable. If we had been working on adding two-digit numbers for the past two weeks, it was likely that we would add the numbers that appeared in the word problems. We often didn't need to figure out what to do because it was directly related to the computations we had been practicing. Word problems got a bad name as they were often not *problems* at all, since the skill was immediately recognizable and the solutions simple to find.

In today's math classrooms, we have expanded and extended our concept of problem solving. Today's word problems strive to push students' thinking with problems that represent more complex situations, require more thinking to find solutions and even may result in multiple answers. They may be short or long, but always push students to think to find a solution. Some are certainly more complex than others; however, even simple problems can be meaningful and present foundational skills that will later serve our students well as they attempt to solve complex problems. The term *word problems* does not have to be applied only to the traditional types we experienced. Problems are in words, because words express ideas and present situations. In equations, the numbers and symbols are written out for us, telling us which operation to use and on which numbers we should be using it. That makes it a rote process. In word problems, the words provide us with a situation and we must decide which data are important, what we are being asked to do, and how we will proceed to find a solution. It is the words that make it challenging and that invite us to think beyond rote. And it is through words (discussions and writing) that we are able to teach and explore the problem situations. Rather than the traditional word problem—*Janie had 3 apples and 6 pears. How many pieces of fruit did she have?*—today's students will also see problems that challenge them to think more creatively. Consider the following word problem:

Janie has 9 pieces of fruit. She has apples and pears. How many apples and pears could she have?

To find the solution, students must understand that the question is asking them to find a possible combination of apples and pears that will total 9 pieces of fruit. They might use addition or draw a picture to represent the data. They might find multiple solutions to the problem. Our goal is to balance simple tasks with more complex or extended tasks in order to continue to challenge students' thinking. Whether we call them word problems, story problems, or simply problem-solving activities, they are tasks in which the solution is not immediately apparent and students are challenged to think and to apply their math skills (see Figure 2–2). In the following chapters, we explore critical strategies that support students to solve simple as well as increasingly complex problems.

C L A S S R O O M - T E S T E D   T I P

Math Mad-Libs

Connect problem solving to your students' lives and interests with some fun problem-solving mad-libs. Ask students to provide you with some words and numbers to insert into your math problems.

You might ask for a number from 1 to 10, an animal, and an animal body part, for example. Then insert the students' responses in your mad-lib problem:

Example: There were ____ (number from 1 to 10) ____ (kind of animal). How many _____ (body parts–e.g., ears, eyes, legs) were there?
 There were <u>4</u> <u>pigs</u>. How many <u>ears</u> were there?
 There were <u>3</u> <u>cows</u>. How many <u>legs</u> were there?

Make the problems as simple or as challenging as necessary for your students. Do mad-libs as a whole-class activity asking different students to share a response to fill in each blank. They will have so much fun filling in the blanks to create the problems that they will be begging you to do mad-lib problem-solving again soon!

Figure 2–2 *This student is challenged to apply her math understanding to solve a real problem about the number of jellybeans in a bowl.*

Questions for Discussion

1. How do the word problems you remember from your days as a student compare to the word problems that you see in math textbooks today?

2. How can attention to the steps of the problem-solving process support students as they attempt to solve problems?

3. What are some key instructional techniques to help students recognize effective problem-solving thinking?

4. Many students get stuck during their attempts to solve problems. What tips for getting "unstuck" might be helpful to them? How might these ideas be shared?

3

Focusing on Problem-Solving Strategies

As with any other component of the mathematical tool kit, strategies must receive instructional attention if students are expected to learn them.

—National Council of Teachers of Mathematics,
Principles and Standards for School Mathematics

For some of our students, thinking skills come easily. These students are naturally able to organize ideas, represent concepts, adjust predictions, and draw conclusions. For many others, exposure to, experience with, and reflection about their thinking is vital. It may be difficult for them to determine where to begin working on a problem, how to simplify a problem, or how to effectively move through the problem to a solution. While one student might view a problem as easy, another sees the same problem as difficult and is unable to determine an approach that will lead him or her to the answer. Many students judge problems as difficult or confusing only because they lack the skills to plan an approach, organize the ideas, and ultimately, simplify the problem. Knowledge of problem-solving strategies provides our students with the tools to simplify problems.

The Importance of Problem-Solving Strategies

Problem-solving strategies are what we do in our heads as we make sense of and solve problems. They are our tools for simplifying problems and revealing the possible paths to solutions. Focusing on the development of problem-solving strategies is about helping students understand and employ sound thinking processes, an important goal of mathematics instruction. It is the understanding of these thinking processes, combined with a knowledge of math skills and an understanding of math concepts, that allows our students to effectively solve problems. As our students are challenged to solve problems about measurement, their understanding of the concept of measurement and their knowledge of various units of measurement are important, but without the thinking skills to analyze the problem situation and determine which numbers to use and which operation to apply, students would be unable to find a solution. The better our students understand their own thinking and continue to develop that thinking, the more confident they are during problem-solving tasks. This focus on understanding their own thinking (metacognition) is a critical goal of good problem-solving instruction.

Much has been written about the teaching of problem-solving strategies. While there are some variations in the names of the strategies, there is much agreement regarding the critical-thinking skills that play a key role in math problem solving, and therefore deserve attention in our math classrooms. The names that have been given to the key problem-solving strategies are simple and are intended to capture the essence of the thinking skills (Choose an Operation; Find a Pattern; Make a Table; Make an Organized List; Draw a Picture or Diagram; Use Logical Reasoning; Guess, Check, and Revise; and Work Backward). Even though the names are quite simple, we should not assume that these skills are simple. While they can be presented in a simple form to young students, they continue to develop in complexity and support students at all grade levels as they attempt to solve even the most complex of problems.

Beneath the simple strategy names lie an array of important skills that empower students to be more effective problem solvers. Good problem solvers understand the operations and can recognize them in problem situations (Choose an Operation). Good problem solvers observe numbers and recognize connections between numbers (Find a Pattern, Make a Table). Good problem solvers can organize data to work through problems in systematic ways (Make a Table, Make an Organized List, Draw a Picture or Diagram). Good problem solvers can use inverse thinking when necessary to find a solution (Work Backward). Good problem solvers can make sense of a seeming overload of information and can organize it and draw conclusions from it (Draw a Picture or Diagram, Use Logical Reasoning). Good problem solvers take risks and use their number sense combined with trial-and-error thinking to proceed toward a solution (Guess, Check, and Revise). The simple problem-solving strategies are not simple at all, but represent significant thinking skills. Students who become adept at these thinking skills are armed with the tools they need to face many and varied problems.

As we explore problem-solving strategies throughout this book, it is important to remember that we are not teaching or telling students to use a particular strategy, but rather helping them develop the thinking skills to find an appropriate strategy for solving a problem. Often more than one strategy will lead to a solution. Students' work should be evaluated based on the reasonableness of the strategy, not whether it was the strategy we may have had in mind as we posed the problem. Consider the following problem:

There was 1 dog, 2 pigs, 3 chickens, 4 cows, 5 ducks, and 6 kittens on the farm. How many animals were on the farm?

The student work samples in Figures 3–1 and 3–2 show different, but both appropriate, strategies for solving the problem. While one student used addition to find the solution, the other drew a diagram and counted to find the answer. Sharing the varied ways that students solve problems enlightens others in the class to possible methods. As we help students recognize and employ varied problem-solving approaches we are helping them build a repertoire of problem-solving strategies, which is the utimate goal for each of our students (NCTM 1989).

C L A S S R O O M - T E S T E D   T I P

Problem-Solving Journals

Math journals are a nice way to promote reflection about problem solving. A weekly problem might be posed for students to solve in their math journals. In primary grades, the teacher might simply provide each student with a problem to glue into their journals and then ask them to solve it and write about the solution. Students can then be asked to share their work with a partner or to share their solution with the class during a group sharing.

Some teachers like to have students record a demonstration problem for each strategy in their journal—one that was discussed and solved with the whole class. The journals then become a place for "familiar" problems—those benchmark problems that students explored together—and remind students of a problem that illustrates each strategy .

Problem-solving journals are a great way to document students' progress in the development of problem-solving skills. They make handy artifacts for parent conferences or workshops and allow parents to view the types of problems their children are exploring, as well as provide a glimpse into their own child's strengths and weaknesses. And they are a wonderful way for students to see their own progress over the course of the school year.

[*Note:* Marble composition books make good math journals, but a journal does not have to be a bound book—it can be a collection of pages that teachers bind for students (see the journal/writing pages on the CD).]

Keys to Developing Strategies

Within a single classroom, students' abilities to understand and apply strategies may differ dramatically. While some students intuitively apply the strategies, others may be at a beginning level in their understanding. These strategies do not develop by grade level, but by experience with and exposure to this type of thinking. A first-grade student who has had opportunities to explore and discuss the strategies may show greater development than a second-grade student who has had limited exposure to this type of thinking. An understanding of the development of these strategies from simple to complex benefits teachers at all grade levels and provides us with crit-

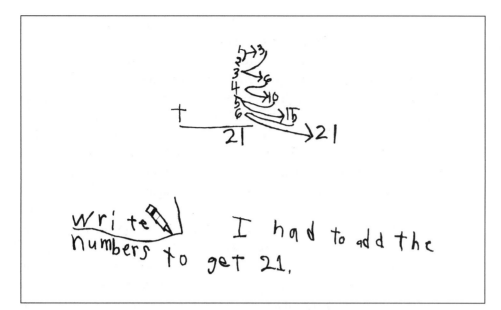

Figure 3–1 *Kyle recorded each number and then added the numbers to find the sum.*

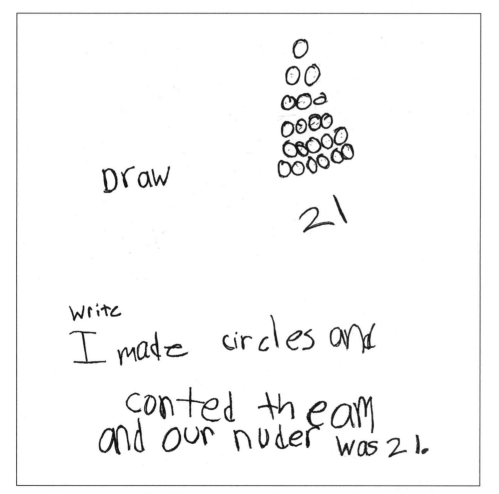

Figure 3–2 *Maggie used circles to represent each animal and then counted to find the total.*

ical knowledge to adjust our instruction. With a deep understanding of these strategies, we are able to break down the skills to support our struggling students or layer on sophistication to challenge our more proficient problem solvers.

Attention to the development of problem-solving strategies begins in the primary grades. As students progress through the grades, these thinking skills are refined and enhanced. While kindergarten students might explore organized lists through simple problems about combinations between two kinds of cookies and two kinds of juice, second-grade students might explore organized lists through more sophisticated tasks like finding the different combinations of coins that would equal 25 cents. The essential thinking skills (finding a systematic way to move through the data and record the information) are similar, but the latter problem is more complex, requiring additional thought. Facility with problem-solving strategies does not develop in a single lesson, but rather continues to develop over the years as students experience and explore problems of increasing sophistication. Understanding the progression of these skills, from simple to complex, allows teachers to effectively meet students' needs and help them refine and extend their understanding of each strategy. As you explore the practice problems on the CD you will notice the increasing complexity within each set of problems and will be able to differentiate lessons by choosing problems based on the needs of your students.

In prekindergarten through second grade, we introduce each strategy in a simple form. While some students may intuitively use some of these strategies, they may not recognize their thinking. Beginning at a simple level will help students experience success and will provide an opportunity to discuss the underlying thinking skills. Visual or hands-on activities are particularly useful in helping students visualize each strategy.

Once students have been introduced to each strategy, frequent practice tasks provide opportunities for them to revisit the skills. Quality is better than quantity in practice sessions, as we place more emphasis on talking through a few problems than on simply completing many problems. Questions such as "How did you solve that problem?" "What strategy did you use?" "How did you know to use that strategy?" and "What was confusing about that problem and what did you do to make it easier?" will begin to focus students on their thinking. Prompting our students to think about similar problems by asking "When have we seen something like this before?" or "Does this problem remind you of any you have done before?" will help them improve their skills in selecting appropriate strategies.

Getting students talking about these problem-solving strategies is important. Students' metacognitive skills increase as they are challenged to think about and express their own thinking. Students should have frequent opportunities to work in groups to talk about problem-solving tasks (see Figure 3–3), and should be asked frequently to explain, justify, and reflect on their problem solving.

Ask students to explain how they solve problems:

- List the steps you used to solve this problem.

- Explain how you solved this problem.

- What might be another way to solve this problem?

Figure 3–3 *These students work together to discuss a class problem.*

Ask students to justify their answers or their decisions:

■ Which strategy did you choose? Why do you think that strategy was a good choice for solving this problem?

■ Why do you believe your answer is correct?

■ Explain why you set up your (table, diagram, list, etc.) the way you did.

Ask students to write problems of their own:

■ Write a problem that can be solved using addition (or subtraction).

■ Write a problem that can be solved by using a table (or finding a pattern or drawing a picture, etc.).

■ Write a problem about 10 + 25.

Ask students to reflect on their strengths, weaknesses, and feelings as they learn problem solving

■ What was easy about solving this problem? What was hard?

■ What are you still confused about? Do you have any questions that need to be answered?

- What did you do when you got stuck?

- What did you discover?

- What will you do next time?

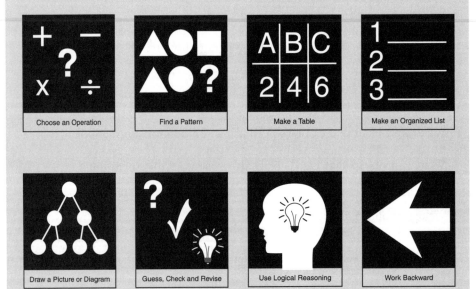

CLASSROOM-TESTED TIP

Problem-Solving Icons

As students attempt to select an appropriate strategy for solving a problem, the use of icons (pictures to represent the strategies) can help to remind them of the strategies they have explored in class (see Figure 3–4). A bulletin board or special area of the classroom can be designated to display the icons. As students are introduced to a specific strategy, an icon for that strategy is posted. Additional icons are posted as students build their repertoire of strategies. Throughout the year, as students attempt to solve problems, the teacher can direct their attention to the icons as reminders of possible solution strategies. See Strategy Icons on the CD for reproducible icons to post in your classroom or Strategy Bookmarks on the CD for a template to create math bookmarks that display the icons for student reference during class or homework assignments.

Choose an Operation	Find a Pattern	Make a Table	Make an Organized List
Draw a Picture or Diagram	Guess, Check and Revise	Use Logical Reasoning	Work Backward

Figure 3–4 *Icons posted in the classroom remind students of possible strategies for solving math problems.*

What's in a Name?

Through teacher talk and think-alouds, student-to-student discussions about problems, whole-class debriefings after problem solving, and opportunities to write about their insights and experiences, students begin to hear each other's ideas and practice expressing their own. During these communication activities the simple strategy names (e.g., Find a Pattern, Use Logical Reasoning, Guess and Check) serve to support our students who now have words to express the abstract thinking processes they are experiencing. One second grader, when asked to explain how she got her answer, exclaimed, "I used logical reasoning." "What do you mean?" the teacher asked. "It said his shape had more than 4 sides and a triangle only has 3 and a square and a rectangle don't have more than 4 sides, they just have 4 sides, so I knew it must be a pentagon! I used my logic!" This simple strategy name allowed her to find words to label and describe her thinking processes.

CLASSROOM-TESTED TIP

Problem-Solving Circles

Following problem-solving activities, students might be asked to share their solutions during circle time. During this time, students sit in a circle so that everyone can see as classmates share their ideas and hold up their written work. Circle time introduces students to different ways of solving problems and gives the teacher an opportunity to hear students' thinking about the problems. Some teachers like having a special "sharing chair" in which the student who is sharing can sit as he explains his work.

Exploring the Strategies in Detail

While most textbooks and curricula contain problems focused on these strategies, assigning these problem tasks will not teach these skills. It is the selection of problems combined with discussion, exploration, and reflection that supports students as they develop an understanding of problem-solving strategies. While we were all assigned problems, we were not all taught how to solve math problems. The way in which we introduce, explore and illustrate the strategies can greatly support the development of our students' skills. In the following chapters, we explore each strategy in more detail. We look at visual, hands-on, and interactive ways to present, explore, and discuss a variety of problem-solving strategies so that students will be able to understand and apply the strategies to make sense of and solve a wide range of math problems.

Questions for Discussion

1. In what ways can students benefit from understanding their own thinking (metacognition) and recognizing which problem-solving strategies they are using?

2. Why is it important to help students build a repertoire of strategies?

3. What is the role of communication (talk and writing) in developing problem-solving strategies?

4. Why might it be important for a teacher to understand the progression of skills in these problem-solving strategies?

CHAPTER 4

Strategy

Choose an Operation

Understanding the fundamental operations of addition, subtraction, multiplication, and division is central to knowing mathematics. One essential component of what it means to understand an operation is recognizing conditions in real-world situations that indicate that the operation would be useful in those situations.

—National Council of Teachers of Mathematics,
Curriculum and Evaluation Standards for School Mathematics

We know the importance of helping our students understand the problem-solving process—the way to proceed through a problem from start to finish. We recognize that our students must be able to identify the question being asked before they can effectively find a solution. But we also recognize that once students know what they are being asked to solve, they must be able to consider varied approaches and decide on a plan that makes sense for that problem. Addition and subtraction, and possibly multiplication, are methods many primary students use to find the solution to math problems. Determining which operation is appropriate for solving a problem is a critical, and frequently used, problem-solving strategy.

Students will be better able to select the appropriate operation to solve a problem if they have a deep understanding of the operations. It is critical that primary students have many experiences in which they explore the operations of addition and subtraction. Demonstrations, explanations, and hands-on experiences during the introduction of each operation help our students understand the concepts of addition and subtraction and provide a strong foundation for using these operations to solve problems.

About Math Operations

It is important that our students learn how to add and subtract, but to be effective problem solvers they also need to recognize *when* to add or subtract. Understanding math operations is more than simply knowing how to perform calculations; it is understanding when each operation makes sense to solve a problem. Rather than focusing on abstract numbers, it is critical that we introduce primary students to math operations with a focus on the meanings of those operations.

Addition

Addition is the process of joining things together. The sets do not have to be equal. Rather than focusing on the key word *altogether*, keep in mind that it is the concept of *altogether* (bringing groups together or joining parts to make a whole), not the word, that tells a student that it is time to add. If we know how many girls are in the classroom and how many boys are in the classroom, we can add to find the total number of children in the classroom.

In the early grades, students might draw and count items (e.g., 4 cats and 6 dogs), but as they develop addition skills they are able to use the operation to solve the problem in a more abstract way (e.g., 4 + 6). Addition is an appropriate operation to use to find out the total number of items even if each group is equal. Through repeated addition students might determine that there are 12 plates if they know that there are 4 red plates, 4 blue plates, and 4 yellow plates. Through repeated addition (4 + 4 + 4) or skip counting (e.g., 4, 8, 12), they are able to find a solution, although they will later discover a more efficient method as multiplication is introduced.

In the primary grades, we help students understand addition as we place groups of objects on the overhead and physically pull them together, or as we use physical demonstrations in the classroom, joining groups of boys and girls to find the number of students to illustrate this *joining* concept. Our students benefit greatly from hands-on experiences and visual demonstrations as they develop their understanding of the operation of addition.

Subtraction

Subtraction can be more difficult for students to understand than addition because there are several models for subtraction. The most commonly taught is the *take-away* or *separate* model. Whenever something is removed from a group or separated from the group, we subtract. Students pick this concept up quickly. If there were 10 pieces of candy in a bag and we ate 3 of them, subtraction would help us find out how many pieces of candy were left in the bag.

Another very important model for subtraction is the *compare* model. Whenever quantities are compared, we use subtraction to find the *difference* between them. If we are asking students to determine how much taller, wider, or heavier one object is than another, they would need to subtract to find the difference. Helping our students visualize the comparison will help them better understand this model. Students might be asked to create trains using connecting blocks and then compare them by lining them up side by side. Students can see and count how much longer one train is than the other. Using overhead counters is another way to help students visualize this concept. Another phrase often used in subtraction problems asks a child to determine *how many more* of something are needed to make two quantities equal. This is a form of comparison. For example, a comparison problem could read:

If Katie had 14 stickers and Michael had 10 stickers, how many more stickers did Katie have?

Using stickers (or manipulatives to represent the stickers) and lining the two rows next to each other will allow students to see the difference between the two groups and help them visualize this comparison model.

Multiplication

While most primary students do not receive instruction in multiplication, some begin to discover it as they explore problems with repeated addition. When quantities are the same (e.g., $3 + 3 + 3$), multiplication becomes a more efficient way to find the answer. The concept of multiplication can be demonstrated with real objects, manipulatives, or overhead materials. Like addition, multiplication is used to find the total number of objects (the whole); however, when using multiplication, all sets have the same number of objects. If there are 6 packs of cupcakes and each pack has 2 cupcakes in it, multiplication can be used to find the total number of cupcakes (e.g., 6×2). Using manipulatives to construct equal groups and then pulling the groups together on an overhead or on students' desktops will visually demonstrate the concept of joining equal sets. Connecting multiplication to addition concepts and showing its connection to skip counting can help our students develop a deeper understanding of the operation.

Division

Although students in the primary years are generally not taught division, they do begin to recognize the model of separating a whole into equal groups or of fair sharing. Through children's literature (e.g., *The Doorbell Rang* by Pat Hutchins) or through story problems (e.g., dividing candy fairly between friends), students can begin to develop an understanding of division so they are ready to apply that understanding to the problems they will face in the intermediate grades. And as they begin to learn about fractions, students will be exposed to this concept of dividing a whole into equal groups.

Hands-On Introduction to Operations

Good problem solvers understand math operations. Help your students *see* addition and subtraction scenarios by providing a variety of visual demonstrations. As you demonstrate the take-away (separate) model for subtraction using the overhead projector, create various problem situations so students hear a variety of scenarios to illustrate the operation (e.g., dogs running out of a yard, birds flying away, cookies being eaten). It is helpful to mark a circle on the overhead and place the original group (the whole) inside the circle. As you take away (the part), students will see you remove the objects from the circle but will still be able to see them on the projection screen. They are then able to count how many have been taken from the group (one part) and how many still remain (the other part).

Using an overhead projector also provides a simple but effective way to view the comparison model for subtraction. By placing two rows of counters or tiles next to each other, and then having students count to see the difference between the rows, students can visualize this comparison model.

Key Words Versus Key Concepts

Even though teachers often use key words as a method of assisting students in choosing an appropriate operation, be careful to avoid teaching students to rely solely on key words (Sowder 2002). It is often true that when the word *altogether* appears in a problem, it is an addition problem. The word *altogether* can appear in other problems, however, and students who look for one or two familiar words but do not stop to *think about* the problem situation may incorrectly determine that addition is the operation to use. Consider the following problem:

> Jackie had some chocolate cookies and some peanut butter cookies. She had 12 cookies altogether. She ate 4 of them. How many cookies did she have left?

While the word *altogether* does appear, it is not an indication that addition should be used, as this is clearly a subtraction problem. Asking students to think about what is happening in the problem (some cookies in a group were eaten) will help them determine that subtraction is the appropriate operation. Words sometimes appear within a problem that may mislead students who are relying only on finding a key word.

Students should look for *key concepts* rather than *key words*. After reading the problem, they should visualize the situation rather than focusing on a word or phrase in hopes that it will tell them how to proceed. You might ask students to close their eyes and think about the problem. Are objects being joined? Is something being taken away from a group? Are objects being compared to see which is shorter, longer, or taller? Understanding the key concepts for each operation will help students make a thoughtful decision regarding the appropriate operation to use in solving the problem.

CLASSROOM-TESTED TIP

Pinch Cards

Pinch cards, a form of all-pupil response, also provide practice in identifying the correct operation. All students receive their own card. While first graders will work with a card that has only addition and subtraction operation signs, some more advanced second graders may be ready for a card that also includes a multiplication sign. Teachers can create their own cards, being sure to duplicate the operation signs on both sides of the cards, or use the Pinch Cards samples on the CD. The operation signs should be placed in the same location on the front and back of the card, so students can see the sign from the back of the card while teachers see the same sign from the front. As the teacher poses a problem, students pinch (hold the card by that sign) the operation they would use to solve the problem. The teacher then briefly asks students to justify their decisions. This allows a quick, interactive review that students enjoy, and it allows teachers to quickly spot those students who are still having difficulty with the concepts. Those students may be pulled aside later for review or reteaching.

Developing the Skill of Choosing the Correct Operation

Hands-On and Visual Experiences with Operations

Visual demonstrations and hands-on experiences help make the operations understandable to primary students. Teachers might display objects on an overhead projector and demonstrate the action of joining or separating objects while talking about the ideas. Teachers might allow students to act out addition or subtraction scenarios, recording the correlating equations on the board for students to see. Teachers might use number lines to help students visualize the concepts, or provide students with manipulatives (e.g., square tiles, colored counters) to allow them opportunities to explore the operations in a hands-on way. Repeated opportunities to act out or visualize addition and subtraction problems will help students better understand each operation.

Connect Operations to Daily Classroom Activities

Allow students to experience addition and subtraction through everyday classroom activities. Add the number of chairs at two tables in the classroom. Subtract to find out how many more crayons are in one package than another. Add the number of boys and girls to find out how many students are in line. Pose problems about lunch boxes, pencils, backpacks, or glue sticks to allow students to continually see examples of problem situations that can be solved using math operations.

Operations in Context Through Children's Literature

A fun and engaging way to support students' understanding of operations is through children's literature. Many stories show math operations in a motivating and memorable way. Students are able to talk about the operations as they relate them to the characters and actions in the story. In *Rooster's Off to See the World* by Eric Carle, a rooster sets off to see the world and 14 animals join him along the way. Students can add as more and more animals join the rooster, and then subtract as animals decide to go home (leave the group). In *Five Little Monkeys Jumping on the Bed by* Eileen Christelow, students hear the fun subtraction story of monkeys who one by one fall off the bed and bump their heads, and in *Monster Math by* Grace Maccarone students experience subtraction with loveable monsters.

Listening to math stories can help lay a foundation for an understanding of multiplication and division. In *Stacks of Trouble by* Martha F. Brenner, the main character, Mike, finds out how quickly stacks of dirty dishes can pile up (multiplication) when he tries to avoid washing them. And while primary students may not learn division computations, they can begin to develop the concept of division by hearing stories like *The Doorbell Rang* by Pat Hutchins in which cookies are shared fairly or *Clean-Sweep Campers by* Lucille Recht Penner in which messy campers try to figure out how to divide themselves into equal teams to clean their bunks. Stories allow students to see scenarios in which the operations are used. Discussing these scenarios, and relating them to math operations, helps to strengthen our students' understanding of the operations.

C L A S S R O O M - T E S T E D   T I P

Addition and Subtraction Stories

Reading math stories to your students helps them see examples of addition and subtraction in context. Try some of the following stories to jump-start discussions about these operations.

Addition

Carle, Eric. 1972. *Rooster's Off to See the World*. New York: Scholastic.
DeRubertis, B. 1999. *A Collection for Kate*. New York: Kane Publishing.
Ehlert, L. 1992. *Fish Eyes*. New York: Voyager Books.

Merriam, E. 1993. *12 Ways to Get to 11*. New York: Simon and Schuster Books.
Murphy, S. J. 1998. *Animals on Board*. New York: HarperCollins.
Murphy, S. J. 2001. *Safari Park*. New York: HarperCollins.
Walsh, E. S. 1991. *Mouse Count*. New York: Harcourt Brace & Co.

Subtraction

Carle, E. 1972. *Rooster's Off To See the World*. New York: Scholastic.
Christelow, E. 1989. *Five Little Monkeys Jumping on the Bed*. New York: Clarion
  Books.
Ernst, L. C. 1995. *Up to Ten and Down Again*. New York: HarperTrophy.
Maccarone, G. 1995. *Monster Math*. New York: Scholastic.
Wise, W. 1993. *Ten Sly Piranhas*. New York: Scholastic.

Group Activities and Discussions

It is important for students to have opportunities to talk about which operation makes sense for a specific scenario. Pair and group activities in which students are given a problem and asked to work together to determine the correct operation are critical. As students discuss which operation they would choose and why, they are able to hear each other's ideas and strengthen their understanding of the key concepts. When sharing their answers with the rest of the class, students should be asked why they chose the operation they did.

Student-Created Problems

Asking students to develop their own problems is another way to help them strengthen their skills at understanding the operations. Students might be asked to work with partners to:

Write a problem about 4 + 6.
Write a problem in which you have to add to get the answer.
Write a problem about candy that was eaten.

Working with partners allows students to talk through the situation and support each other. After students write their story problems, have them present the problems to their group or to the entire class. The class might try to solve their problem, or students might be asked to sort the problems by operation. Asking students to explain how they knew which operation they should use to solve each problem helps us to understand their thinking process.

CLASSROOM-TESTED TIP

Writing Story Problems

Using equations to prompt students to write story problems is an effective way to assess students' understanding of the basic operations. Provide students with an equation and ask them to create a story problem to match the equation. Consider the following equation:

$$10 + 21 = 31$$

Story: Katie bought some candy. She bought 10 chocolate kisses and 21 peppermints. How many pieces of candy did she buy altogether?

There are lots of other stories that might go with the same equation.

Another story: There were 10 daisies and 21 roses in Mrs. Alexander's garden. How many flowers were in her garden?

Students can write their stories in math journals or share their stories aloud with their group or the whole class. With a thumbs-up or fist (no thumb up) response, classmates can indicate whether the story matches the equation. If stories don't match the equation, classmates can suggest ways to rewrite the story to make it fit. Writing story problems helps students strengthen their understanding of the operations.

Supporting Students in Solving More Complex Problems

While some primary problems are very simple, others contain challenging components that can cause frustration for some students. Understanding what makes some problems more complex will help us find ways to support struggling students. Even in the primary grades, we see problems that contain unnecessary information, problems that require students to select appropriate data, multi-step problems, and even problems that require students to understand additional math concepts or vocabulary. Finding ways to help our students deal with the complexity of problems is an important responsibility of teachers of problem solving.

Even in the primary grades, students are often faced with finding the data they need to solve a problem. Sometimes unnecessary data are presented in the problem and students must determine what is needed and what is not needed to find a solution. The following problem contains unnecessary information:

Jill had 10 eggs in her basket. She had 4 yellow eggs and 6 green eggs. How many more green eggs did she have?

In order to find out how many more green eggs she had, we simply have to subtract (6 − 4). It is not necessary that we know how many total eggs she had, and 10 is not necessary data for solving the problem. The ability to identify unnecessary information is a critical problem-solving skill. Students need to be able to understand the question being asked and to identify the data that specifically address that question. Focusing on identifying unnecessary information is essentially focusing on whether students *know the question* and *know the data needed to find an answer*. Asking students to state what they are trying to find out and what they already know helps to focus them on the connection between the data and the question. Teachers might ask students to cross out unnecessary data in the problem. Asking them to clarify why the data are not needed helps ensure their understanding.

Students might be asked to select data from a set of data in order to solve a problem. Consider the following problem, which asks students how much it costs to buy a cookie and a glass of milk.

Students must use the list of data to locate the appropriate data for solving the problem.

Snacks

Cookie	20 cents
Candy	10 cents
Cupcake	15 cents
Lemonade	30 cents
Milk	20 cents

Students must now select the needed data from a set of data and then combine (add) the price of the milk and cookie in order to find the answer.

Even in the primary grades, students may be faced with multi-step problems. Consider the following problem:

Kelly has 2 dimes and 3 nickels. How much money does she have?

There are several steps for solving this problem. Students might first figure out that 2 dimes is 20 cents, and then figure out that 3 nickels is 15 cents, and finally, add 20 cents and 15 cents to get a total of 35 cents. Multi-step problems may require students to apply more than one math skill as they solve the problem. Along with understanding the operation of addition, this problem challenges students to apply their understanding of the value of coins. When initially posing multistep tasks, it may be helpful to split the task into parts and then guide students as they move from step to step. This helps some students gain confidence as well as develop their understanding of the multistep process. And providing opportunities for students to discuss and write about the steps they took to solve multi-step problems is critical. Having students record the process in a numbered list will help focus them on the steps of the process.

1. I found that 2 dimes is 20 cents.

2. I found that 3 nickels is 15 cents.

3. I added 20 cents and 15 cents and got 35 cents.

Some primary problems are complicated by the need for students to understand additional math concepts or vocabulary. Consider the following problem:

Danny's soccer team ate 1 dozen chocolate cookies. They also ate 7 sugar cookies. How many cookies did they eat altogether?

To solve this problem, students need to understand the question and how the data in the question (e.g., a dozen cookies) differs from the data being asked for in the solution (e.g., individual cookies). And they will need to use their understanding of the concept of a dozen to find the solution. The use of the term *dozen* adds to the complexity of the task While this problem provides a challenge for some students, we must remember that our ulitimate goal is to help our students effectively solve these types of problems. We can support students by remaining focused on modeling good thinking and by offering many opportunities for students to explore challenging problems. Continually asking "What do we need to find out?" "What do we know?" "How will the data help us?" "What steps should we take to find the solution?" and "Does our answer match the question?" will help students focus on key questions to drive their problem-solving experiences. And frequent and specific feedback will provide students with insight into where they might be going off-track or ways to rethink a problem to more effectively get to the solution.

A Look at Student Work

The following student comments illustrate their reasoning regarding choosing an appropriate operation. In each case, students analyzed the problem situation and chose the operation based on their understanding of the problem, not their identification of key words that appeared in the problem.

Kara went to the zoo. She saw 3 tigers, 4 polar bears, and 6 lions. How many animals did she see?
    "You add because she saw them all. You just put them together." (This student recognized the concept of addition.)

Fifteen children were swimming in the pool. Five got out because they were cold. How many were still in the pool?
    "I subtracted because some got out of the pool. You have to take them away." (Notice the understanding of subtraction.)

John had 24 goldfish crackers and Grady had 14. How many more did John have?

"You can subtract or you can just line them up and see which is more." (Notice the idea of subtraction as comparing the two groups.)

Allison made 4 bracelets. Each bracelet had 10 beads on it. How many beads did Allison use to make the bracelets?

"I added 10 + 10 + 10 + 10, but they're all the same so you could just count 10, 20, 30, 40." (Notice the connection between addition and skip-counting.)

Communicating About the Strategy

Asking students to talk and write about how they arrived at an answer or why they selected an operation helps teachers better assess their understanding of the operations. Allowing students to work in pairs or groups to discuss their choice of operations will help them begin to develop ways to verbalize their thoughts. By listening to others and sharing ideas, they begin to find the words they need to explain their math thinking. And for students who are able to write, it is important to encourage them to put their math thoughts in writing both to support the development of their thinking and to help us better assess their understanding. Even those students who may require the use of pictures or diagrams to support their explanations will benefit from attempts to "explain their thinking."

Following are some discussion or writing prompts to extend students' thinking about operations:

- What operation did you use to solve this problem? Why?

- Explain the steps you used to solve this problem.

- Prove your answer.

- How did you decide on the number sentence you used to solve this problem?

Selecting Practice Problems

Practice problems using addition and subtraction are available in any math book. Students need practice with identifying operations and building appropriate equations to represent problem situations. And continuing to increase the complexity of the problem tasks through the introduction of more complex problems (e.g., problems with unnecessary information) will help develop and refine your students' problem-solving skills. While these problems can be found in textbooks, keep in mind that creating problems that connect math to events and situations in your students' lives will motivate and excite them. Simply rewording textbook problems to include your students' names or the names of local stores, parks, or schools will help to personalize the problem-solving experience. The practice problems provided on the accompanying CD can be modified on your computer prior to printing them. Add your students'

names or the names of television shows, favorite songs, and local attractions. Seize any opportunity to make a real-world connection for your students.

Questions for Discussion

1. Why is it important for students to understand operations?

2. What is the difference between key words and key concepts?

3. How can visual and hands-on activities support students' understanding of operations?

4. How might children's literature be used to help students understand math operations?

CHAPTER 5

Strategy

Find a Pattern

By continuing to provide a broad variety of opportunities to explore and use patterns, we help students move from a basic recognition of patterns to a more sophisticated use of patterns as a problem-solving strategy.

—Terrence G. Coburn NCTM *Addenda Series—Patterns*

Patterns are central to our number system. Students begin to recognize and repeat patterns early in their mathematics education. This ability to understand, identify, and extend patterns helps students solve many math problems.

In the primary grades, students begin to investigate patterns through hands-on experiences. We create sound patterns for our students to echo, such as clap-snap-clap-snap. Students act out patterns as they sit, sit, stand, sit, sit, stand. They work with color cubes to create color patterns like blue-green-green-blue-green-green. As our students internalize the concept that patterns repeat in a predictable way, they are able to continue the patterns, predicting what will come next.

Discovering a Variety of Patterns

Patterns range from simple to very complex. Students in the primary grades are first introduced to patterns with shapes, colors, and simple numbers. They begin to internalize the concept that patterns repeat in a predictable way, and they learn to continue the patterns. Primary students explore varied patterns from ab patterns (red–blue, red–blue, red–blue) to aab patterns (red–red–blue, red–red–blue, red–red–blue) to growing patterns (1–2, 1–2–2, 1–2–2–2, . . .), and as students experiment with patterns, they learn to identify the repeating elements and extend the patterns. In the

47

primary grades, it is important to expose students to a variety of patterns, challenging them to identify the patterns, extend the patterns, and create patterns of their own.

Completing and Describing Number Patterns

Patterns are everywhere in our number system. Beginning with simple patterns and challenging students with increasingly complex number patterns will help them develop a greater understanding of numbers and operations. While many math activities ask students to simply complete a pattern, asking our students to describe patterns extends their thinking and helps us better assess their understanding. Students describe a variety of number patterns below:

> 2, 4, 6, 8 . . .
> *"You count by twos."*
> *"You keep adding two more each time."*

> 25, 20, 15, 10 . . .
> *"You're counting down."*
> *"You take five away."*
> *"It's like counting by fives, but backwards."*
> *"You subtract five each time."*

When asking students to describe patterns, ask several students to share their ideas. Patterns can accurately be described in a variety of ways, and allowing students to hear different descriptions allows them to connect ideas about various operations (e.g., addition, skip-counting, multiplication) and better understand the patterns. When describing the pattern 3, 6, 9, 12 . . . , students might say:

> *"I skip-counted by threes."*
> *"I added 3 to each number."*

Each student has accurately described the pattern, but together, the descriptions show connections between repeated addtion and skip-counting and illustrate important understandings about numbers. And asking students to take a closer look at patterns and to describe the patterns can lead them to interesting, and often unexpected, insights. When asked to describe the pattern 5, 10, 15, 20 . . . , students responded:

> *"It's like counting by fives."*
> *"It's like adding 5 to the one before it."*
> *"Hey, first they end with a 5, then 0, then 5, then 0!" (An interesting insight!)*

The more we ask students to look for patterns within our number system, the more patterns they discover!

Reading Patterns

Encourage students to read patterns to you. When reading patterns, ask students to point to each part of the pattern as they tell you what it is (e.g., square, triangle, square, triangle . . .). By pointing to the parts of the pattern, students become familiar with the order, and by reading the pattern aloud they are able to hear their own thinking and better recognize the repetition. Have students tell you what comes next, and always ask them to justify their answer.

Example: Students read the pattern: 1, 3, 5, 7 . . .

TEACHER: What comes next?
STUDENT: 9 is next.
TEACHER: How do you know?
STUDENT: Because it's like saying all the odd numbers.

Helping Students Recognize Patterns

Primary students may need support in understanding patterns. Providing hands-on experiences, visual support, and encouraging math talk are effective ways to help them recognize the repetition of patterns. Providing hands-on experiences makes the concept of patterns concrete. Giving students colored blocks and having them create and extend color patterns, or providing students with shapes and asking them to create and extend shape patterns make the task interactive, motivating, and concrete. And asking students to "talk" the pattern as they point to the cubes or shapes (e.g., "blue, green, blue, green, blue) will allow them to experience the repetition both by seeing it and hearing it.

Students are greatly supported in understanding number patterns when they are able to visualize them. Using visual tools like number lines and hundred charts helps young students see and recognize number patterns. Students who are able to see 2, 4, 6, 8 circled on a number line, as in Figure 5–1, can share their insights about the "look" of the pattern:

STUDENT: Hey, you skipped one number each time.
TEACHER: So what would be the next number in the pattern?
STUDENT: 10
TEACHER: How do you know?
STUDENT: You have to skip 9, then circle 10.

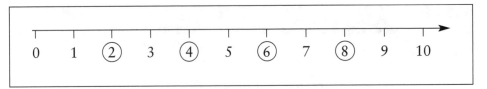

Figure 5–1 *Number lines help students visualize patterns.*

While students might have difficulty recognizing the pattern when seeing just the numbers 2, 4, 6, 8 . . . , seeing it on a number line can bring about an immediate recognition for students who learn best with visual support.

Hundred charts are another valuable tool for allowing students to visualize patterns. Shading in numbers and exploring the resulting pattern helps students gain insights. When exploring 4, 8, 12, 16, we might use a transparent hundred chart on the overhead projector and cover each number in the pattern using colored tiles. This visual allows students to discover that there are three numbers between each tile. In this way, students can predict the next number to be covered. Asking students to describe the patterns they have created will strengthen their observation and communication skills.

"I skipped three squares and then I covered one and then I skipped three squares and then I covered one, and then I did it again. I can just keep skipping three and then covering the next one."

Providing students with their own hundred charts and color tiles will allow them to explore patterns in hands-on ways and further develop their understanding of the repetiton and predictability of patterns. Students will be amazed at the visual patterns that can be created when covering (or coloring) number patterns on a hundred chart (see Figure 5–2). Moving patterns from abstract to visual is a significant tool to support understanding for primary students.

Working with Geometric Patterns

Exploring patterns with geometric figures helps reinforce pattern concepts as well as geometric concepts. Students might explore patterns like the following:

Asking students to describe the pattern (e.g., square, circle, triangle, square, circle, triangle . . .), will provide them with opportunities to explore patterns and reinforce geometry vocabulary.

1	2	3	4	5	6	7	8	9	10
11	12	13	14	15	16	17	18	19	20
21	22	23	24	25	26	27	28	29	30
31	32	33	34	35	36	37	38	39	40
41	42	43	44	45	46	47	48	49	50
51	52	53	54	55	56	57	58	59	60
61	62	63	64	65	66	67	68	69	70
71	72	73	74	75	76	77	78	79	80
81	82	83	84	85	86	87	88	89	90
91	92	93	94	95	96	97	98	99	100

Figure 5–2 *Hands-on explorations with hundred charts help strengthen students' understanding of patterns.*

As students study shapes and record sides and angles, they may begin to recognize more subtle patterns. Second-grade students were asked to predict the next shape in the following pattern:

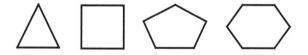

TEACHER: Can someone describe the pattern for me?

STUDENT: It's triangle, square, pentagon, and another one—I don't know the name.

TEACHER: Does anyone know the name of that shape?

STUDENT: I think it's a hexagon.

TEACHER: It is a hexagon. How did you know it was a hexagon?

STUDENT: It has 6 sides.

TEACHER: It does have six sides. So what shape would be next? Turn to your partner and see if you can figure out what might be next.

STUDENT: It's the sides! They have 3 and 4 and 5 and 6!

TEACHER: So how many sides will the next shape have?

STUDENT: Seven!

TEACHER: Does anyone know what we call that shape? *(No one responds.)* It's a heptagon, and it has 7 sides and 7 angles.

The students recognized a pattern after analyzing the shapes, and they found a way to extend the pattern.

Exploring Patterns with Calculators

Primary students enjoy exploring patterns using the calculator's constant function. Students can command the calculator to add 3 or add 6 and then watch the calculator extend the pattern. For addition patterns, have students clear their calculators and press the addition sign, then the number they want added each time (e.g., 2) and then press the equal sign. Each time the equal sign is pressed, the calculator will add 2 (⊞②◻◻◻◻). Students can count aloud as the pattern unfolds. When trying a subtraction pattern, first have students enter a number (e.g., 100), then a subtraction sign, then the number they want to subtract each time, such as 5. Each time they press the equal sign, the calculator will subtract 5 (⑩⓪◻⑤◻◻◻◻◻). You might ask students to predict the number that will be next or to predict whether a number will appear (i.e., If we start with 100 and subtract 5 each time, will we see the number 90? Will we see the number 87? Why?)

Patterns as a Problem-Solving Strategy

Once students become sensitive to searching for patterns, they must be able to recognize them in problem situations. And once a pattern is recognized, students have a plan for how to get to the solution—simply continue the pattern to find the solution. This problem shows a simple pattern embedded in a problem task:

> **Susie was making a necklace with colored beads. She put a red bead on the string, then a blue bead, then a yellow bead, then a red bead, then a blue bead, then a yellow bead. What color bead did she put next?**

Once the pattern is recognized (red, blue, yellow . . .), students can continue it to determine that a red bead would come next. But as always, our goal is to continue to challenge students with increasing complexity. This second part to the problem requires students to apply their understanding of patterns in order to gather the data needed to solve the problem:

> **If Susie put 15 beads on her necklace, how many of each color bead did she use?**

Students now have to continue the pattern until 15 beads have been placed on the necklace and then determine how many of each color will be on the necklace. The recognition and extension of the pattern provides the data needed for solving the problem, but students still must employ their understanding of operations (add to find the number of beads in each color) or their ability to represent the ideas visually (draw a picture of the necklace and count the beads of each color). Patterns become one piece, although a critical piece, to use in solving the problem.

Hands-On Pattern Problems

Beginning by posing simple problems for students to act out and then solve familiarizes them with the use of patterns as a problem-solving strategy. Teachers might give students bear cutouts (see the templates on the CD) of various colors and pose problems like this one:

> The bears marched home for dinner. They were in a line with a blue bear, then a red bear, then a blue bear, then a red bear. Who was next in the line marching home?

In this problem, students were able to use their bear cutouts and simply line them up to see the pattern. Once they recognized the pattern, they simply extended it to find the next bear. In the following problem, the task was made a bit more complex:

> Eight bears marched home for dinner. They lined up with a red bear, then a blue bear, then a red bear, then a blue bear, and so on. Which color bear was at the end of the line?

Now students must line up their bears, recognize the pattern, and follow it to the eighth place to find the solution. Still another variation of the problem might be:

> Eight bears marched home for dinner. They lined up with a green bear, then a blue bear, then a red bear, then a green bear, then a blue bear, then a red bear, and so on. How many red bears were in the line?

While the first problem was simply about recognizing patterns, the other problems challenged students to use their understanding of patterns to find the data needed to solve the problems. Providing students with many opportunities to explore and discuss pattern problems will give them practice using patterns as part of a problem-solving strategy.

A Look at Student Work

Young students can use their understanding of patterns to solve simple problems. Kindergarten students solved problems about the color of cars on a train by creating models using connecting cubes. The teacher told the students the initial colors of the

Figure 5–3 *These kindergarten students extended a color pattern to solve a problem and then checked their answers with a partner.*

cars and asked the students to continue the pattern to find the colors of the remaining cars. Students were asked to check their answers by working with partners and comparing their trains (see Figure 5–3).

As students read and analyze problems, they often recognize a pattern within the data. Recognizing and being able to extend the pattern leads them to a solution. As the student whose work is shown in Figure 5–4 describes the strategy she used to solve the problem, she relates how easy the problem was to solve because she only had to continue the pattern.

Communicating About the Strategy

Asking students to write or talk about creating or extending patterns is a great way to extend their thinking and assess their understanding of patterns. Try prompts like these:

■ Read your pattern to me (talk as you point to each part of the pattern).

■ Describe the pattern.

■ Explain how finding the pattern helped you solve this problem.

■ Is solving problems using patterns easy or hard? Explain your answer.

■ How did an understanding of patterns help you find the data you needed to solve the problem?

Soccer Practice

Katie's soccer coach was trying to get the team in shape for the season. On the first day of practice, she made them run one lap around the field. On the second day, she made them run three laps. On the third day, they ran five laps, and on the fourth day they ran seven laps. How many laps did the coach make them run on the fifth day of practice?

They ran __9__ laps. 1, 3, 5, 7, 9

Describe the pattern. The patern was counting by two's.

How did knowing the pattern help you solve the problem? Knowing the pattern did help me. It was not so hard to do it because I knew how to count by two's.

Figure 5-4 *This student explains how recognizing the
pattern helped her solve the problem.*

■ If a new student entered the room who did not know anything about patterns, how would you explain what they are and how they can help you solve problems? Can you give an example to help them understand?

CLASSROOM-TESTED TIP

Literature Links

Stories are a great way to engage students and set a context for problem-solving activities. In Stuart J. Murphy's *Beep Beep Vroom Vroom!*, patterns come alive. Kevin's sister lines up his toy cars in a variety of ways, setting a context for the exploration of patterns. Read the story to your students and then have them re-enact the story with paper cars (see template on CD). Other stories that set a context for pattern explorations include:

Dee, R. 1988. *Two Ways to Count to Ten*. New York: Henry Holt & Co.
Driscoll, L. 2005. *Super Specs*. New York: The Kane Press.
Kassirer, S. 2001. *What's Next, Nina?* New York: The Kane Press.

Questions for Discussion

1. How does an understanding of patterns help students better understand numbers and operations?

2. How can an understanding of patterns help students solve problems?

3. In what ways might we help primary students understand the concept of patterns?

4. How does a hundred chart or number line support the understanding of patterns? How might they be used in primary classrooms?

Strategy

Make a Table

Organizing data in a table is an essential mathematical skill. It helps children to see relationships within patterns and eventually to generalize these relationships to form a rule.

—Terrence G. Coburn NCTM *Addenda Series—Patterns*

The ability to organize data so that it can be used to solve problems is a critical skill. Tables are one way in which students can organize data in order to see the data more clearly, recognize patterns and relationships within the data, and gain insights about missing data. When making tables, students are challenged to put important problem data in an organized form.

When focusing on the development of this strategy, there are several critical areas to address. Students must understand how to create a table, including which items to list on the table, where to record specific data on the table, and even how to select the correct answer from the many numbers that are recorded on the table. Students must acquire the skills of recognizing and extending patterns and identifying relationships between the numbers on the table in order to interpret the data accurately. And of course, recognizing whether creating a table makes sense to solve a problem is a critical skill. Spending time addressing each of these issues ensures that students have a solid understanding of this strategy.

Understanding the Format of Tables

A foundational skill for using tables is understanding how data can be recorded in rows and columns. Primary students must understand that the data in each row or column are connected to the title or label in that row or column. Presenting simple tables and talking with students about what the data represents is important as students begin to make sense of this way to record data. Consider the following example:

Students	1	2	3	4	5
Gloves	2	4	6	8	10

In this table, the numbers in the top row indicate 1 student, 2 students, 3 students, etc. The label and numbers are connected. The numbers in the bottom row indicate 2 gloves, 4 gloves, 6 gloves, etc. Understanding this format is critical to students' ability to use a table. In addition, students must understand that 1 student connects to 2 gloves in the same way that 2 students connects to 4 gloves. This understanding will help students answer the question: *How many gloves will 5 students have?* Helping primary students understand rows, columns, and the connections between the data are essential preparation for using this strategy.

Teachers who model how to record even simple data in rows or columns are preparing prekindergarten and kindergarten students for the organization skill needed to understand and create tables. We can support students in understanding tables by creating simple tables on the board or overhead, using a think-aloud technique as we describe where we are placing words and numbers. Highlighting rows or columns by placing a colored strip, cut from a colored transparency or plastic folder, over the data focuses young students on that specific row or column of data, while supporting students who might be overwhelmed by too many numbers. Students might be asked to talk with partners to describe data on the tables or to work with a partner to find specific pieces of data. Working together allows students to hear others' ideas and test their own ideas about the table format.

Using Tables to Solve Problems

Tables are a helpful way to organize data. When data are on a table, we often are able to notice patterns in the data, and those patterns can lead us to answers. Consider that when we buy packs of cupcakes at the store, there are two cupcakes in each package. A table like the one that follows can help students find out how many cupcakes they would have if they bought 2, 3, 4, or 5 packages. In this problem, there is a relationship—a connection—between the number of packages and the number of cupcakes, and the table shows that relationship. Every package has 2 cupcakes, so each time one package is added to the top row of the table, two more cupcakes must be added to the corresponding column on the bottom row. By creating a table, students are able to get a better look at the data, use patterns to explore the data, and use the data to solve problems.

Number of packages	1	2	3	4	5
Number of cupcakes	2	4	6	8	10

An important understanding for effectively using tables as a problem-solving strategy is identifying why and in what situations creating a table would make sense to help us find solutions. A critical insight in deciding if a table might be an appropriate strategy is recognizing two items in the problem that have a relationship or a connection, meaning that one item is connected to the other in a predictable way. Teacher modeling, through think-alouds, is an effective way to help students understand the use of tables as a problem-solving strategy. Take the following problem:

Five people can fit in 1 car. If there are 20 people, how many cars will we need?

What do we already know? There is a relationship, a connection, between the number of people and number of cars. Every car fits 5 people. That will always stay the same. Can we figure out how many people can ride in 2 cars based on what we know? How about 3 cars? If I have 1 car, then I can fit 5 people in it. So, if I have 2 cars, then I can fit [5 + 5] or 10 people. If I have 3 cars, I can fit [5 + 5 + 5] or 15 people, and so on. How can we display that data so we can see it more clearly? How about a table on which we can record the data as we figure it out? Talking students through the creation of the table, including discussions about our thinking and the decisions we make as we move toward a solution, is a valuable way to help students develop their skills with this strategy.

To help students develop this skill, we might ask them to read a problem and underline the data that are connected.

To make 1 cake I need 2 eggs. How many eggs do I need to make 4 cakes? (One cake and 2 eggs are connected because I need 2 eggs for every 1 cake.)

Once students begin to recognize the data that are connected, we can demonstrate how to create a table with those items. Have pairs or groups of students practice setting up tables from a series of problems. Working with a partner or team will allow students to hear one another's ideas and will help them learn to recognize that when they see a relationship between items in a problem, creating a table will be an effective way to organize that data so they can see it more clearly.

Once students are able to recognize a table problem and set up the rows, labeled with each item name, students must use the known data to help them complete the remainder of the table. Consider the previous cake problem. Initially, you may need to talk students through each step of the process to determine how many eggs are needed to make 4 cakes. As students think through the problem, "1 cake uses 2 eggs, so 2 cakes use 4 eggs," the data can be recorded on the table. Demonstrating by constructing a table on the blackboard or overhead projector as students talk through the missing data will help them visualize the process.

Number of cakes	1	2
Number of eggs	2	4

With primary students, we might begin by providing tables that are already constructed so we can clarify the way in which the data are arranged on the table. Then we might present a table with some data missing, like the following table, and have students fill in the missing data:

Number of Bags	1	2	3	4	5
Pieces of Candy	3	6	9		

Students are asked to look at the numbers on the table to determine which numbers will complete it. Ultimately, our goal is for students to be able to create their own tables.

It is important to share tables that are both horizontal and vertical. The positioning of the table is not important; it is the organized placement of the data that is important. Show students that the same data can be represented in different ways as long as the data are organized. Modeling some examples for the class while thinking aloud about which data are connected, how to organize the data on a table, and why a table might be helpful will provide students with valuable opportunities to learn how to use tables in problem solving.

CLASSROOM-TESTED TIP

A Hands-On Introduction to Making Tables

Primary students may not understand the numbers on a table. Help them connect the abstract numbers to real objects through class activities like one that follows.

Pose this problem:

Bear stickers cost 5¢ each. How much will 4 bear stickers cost?

Ask students: "What are we trying to find out? What information in the problem will help us?"

Allow students to explore some ways to solve the problem, giving them bear cutouts and nickel coin manipulatives. Ask students to share some of the ways they solved the problem. Begin to demonstrate a possible strategy by creating a table on the overhead projector with overhead coins and overhead bears.

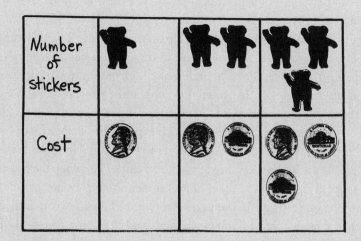

As you fill in the table, ask students to tell you how many coins to place in each section of the table. Continue filling in the table until you find the cost of 4 stickers. Ask students to use their stickers and coins to find the cost of 5 stickers and 6 stickers.

Pose these questions:

"What if we didn't have coins and stickers to help us solve this problem? Is there a way we could use this strategy without the coins and bears?"

Replace the objects with numbers to create a table like the one below. Have students compare the two tables to be sure the values are the same.

Number of stickers	1	2	3	4
Cost	5¢	10¢	15¢	20¢

Ask students:

"Is the answer the same? Do you notice anything about the numbers?"

Discuss the patterns that students see on the table. Ask students if knowing the pattern could help them solve the problem, and if so, how.

Recognizing Patterns and Functions

Although initially students will complete the "Number of eggs" row in the previous problem by adding two eggs each time they add another cake, many will quickly recognize the pattern appearing in the row and simply continue to fill in the numbers as they "count by twos." This recognition of a pattern is an important insight for students and illustrates the power of tables to organize data so that patterns emerge. Sharing observations about patterns will help students recognize the importance of finding a pattern in order to complete tables and, ultimately, solve problems.

Although students may initially see this as a pattern of adding 2 or skip counting by 2, observation and discussion will lead them to discover another relationship between the numbers on the table. Rather than looking horizontally at the patterns that are created, students might notice that when they look at the vertical columns there is a relationship there, too. Students might observe that the number of eggs is always twice the number of cakes. This relationship, which explains the change that is occurring, is called a *function*. As students better understand functions they are able to solve more complex problems. What if I wanted to bake 50 cakes? Knowing the functional relationship of twice as many eggs as cakes allows students to determine that they will need 100 eggs (50 eggs + 50 eggs). The understanding of functions is critical to the study of algebra, and practicing with tables will help students strengthen this skill.

CLASSROOM-TESTED TIP

Guess My Rule

Use In/Out Tables as a quick warm-up activity to help students explore tables and share their insights about the patterns and functions they see. Put a blank table, like the one that follows, on the blackboard, overhead projector, or on chart paper.

IN	OUT

Begin to fill in a value in the "In" column and then place a value in the "Out" column, challenging students to come up with the rule to explain how the "Out" value was determined. Do a few examples and then ask students to turn and share their ideas with a partner to engage all students in discussion about what they are observing. Pairs then share what they believe is the rule. Vary this activity by asking students to work with a partner to develop a rule and then see if the class can guess their rule.

IN	OUT
2	4
3	5
4	6
5	

Rule: Add 2 to the "In" number.

Selecting the Correct Answer

A final stumbling block for using tables to solve problems comes after the table is created. Even if students are able to create the table, they often have a difficult time choosing the correct answer from the many numbers recorded on the table. This is a critical step, since the creation of the table alone does not solve the problem—it only provides the data from which the problem can be solved. Discussions and demonstrations about how to locate the answer among all of the values on the table are essential.

Locating the answer from the data on a table begins with locating the "known" data, which then leads students to the "unknown" data. First, ask students to go back to the question: How many eggs do we need for 4 cakes? Have them locate "4 cakes" on their table and then look for the quantity of eggs that corresponds to that number of cakes. It will be in the same column, directly above or below the 4 cakes on a horizontal table, or will be in the same row, next to the 4 cakes on a vertical table (see the tables below). Teachers might work with a table on an overhead projector or blackboard and place their finger on the number 4 and then move their finger directly down or to the right on the chart to find the matching answer, reminding students that rereading the question to find the "known" information is a key to figuring out where to look for the "unknown" information. Always have students think about and check the answer they have selected to be sure it makes sense.

Number of cakes	1	2	3	4
Number of eggs	2	4	6	⑧

Number of cakes	Number of eggs
1	2
2	4
3	6
4	⑧

CLASSROOM-TESTED TIP

Locating the Answer on a Table

This step can be practiced in an easy, hands-on manner using transparent plastic chips. Refer to the cake problem again. After your students create the table, give each one a chip. Begin to pose questions and ask students to place their chip on the answer from their table. "If I baked 3 cakes, how many eggs would I need?" "If I used 4 eggs, how many cakes did I bake?" As students move their chips to indicate the answer, the teacher walks around the room to assess students' understanding of this skill. An initial demonstration with transparent chips on an overhead projector will help prepare students for the independent practice and will reinforce the skill for students who are still developing their understanding.

Deciding When to Use a Table

With practice, students will be able to create tables, but the ability to construct a table is only a part of the skills they will need. Assisting students in developing the reasoning skill of deciding when this strategy should be used is critical to making it an effective problem-solving tool. After reading a problem that might lend itself to a table, ask students if the problem reminds them of any others they have seen. You might ask them if any of the data go together, as in the cake and eggs problem. Every time we baked a cake, we used 2 eggs. Every time we opened a package of cupcakes, there were 2 cupcakes. Recognizing the connection between two pieces of data alerts us that a table might be an effective way to record and organize the data so that we can see it more clearly. And asking students to justify their choice of strategies will help you see if they've truly mastered not only the mechanics of the skill but the concept of when it is best used.

A Look at Student Work

For young students, we might construct the table, filling in some of the numbers and asking them to look at the table to identify patterns in the data and to continue those patterns to find the answer. The student whose work is shown in Figure 6–1 was able

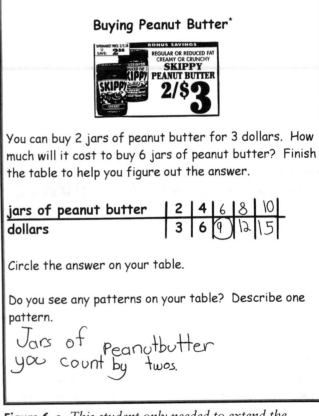

Figure 6–1 *This student only needed to extend the patterns on the table.*

to complete the table, locate the answer on the table, and describe a pattern from the table.

As students become more skilled at completing tables, we might give them less information and ask them to create more of the table on their own. Providing students with only the labels for the rows or columns in the table and asking them to find the numbers from the data in the problem will push their thinking and extend their skills.

Primary students are able to construct their own tables when solving problems. First-grade students were posed the following problem:

There were 5 bags of potatoes on the kitchen table. There were 10 potatoes in each bag. How many potatoes were in all 5 bags?

While some students drew pictures and counted to find the answer, the student whose work is shown in Figure 6–2 constructed her own table and correctly found the number of potatoes, which she circled on the table. Having students share their varied approaches to solving problems can lead to productive class discussions and can help other students see new ways to approach problems. This student shared the table she created to solve the problem. In a similar problem several days later, some of her classmates created tables to solve their problems. A well-facilitated class discussion helps students recognize new approaches for solving problems.

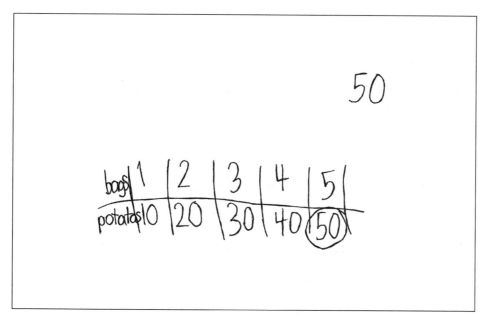

Figure 6–2 *This first-grade student created a table to find the answer to a class problem.*

With practice, students become skilled at creating tables. Asking students to justify their choice of strategies will help you see if they've truly mastered not only the mechanics of the skill, but the concept of when it makes sense for solving a problem. Keep in mind that tables are one way to solve problems and many problems that we might see as "table problems" can be solved in other ways. Our goal is not to require students to use tables, but to build their skills at using tables so they are able to apply this strategy when it is appropriate. As data become more complex in the intermediate grades, tables will become increasingly helpful to organize and analyze problem information.

Learning Through Exploration

Throughout this book we are focusing on assisting all students in developing problem-solving skills and so may decide to introduce strategies (e.g., making tables) to our students in order to stretch their thinking and show them alternate ways to organize math data and solve math problems. We recognize, however, that some of our students may intuitively use these strategies. It is important to be ready to capture that teachable moment as we notice a student using a specific strategy. While most of the class may have drawn pictures to solve a problem, one child may have created a table to show the same data. Encouraging students to share their approaches, and facilitating class discussions about different approaches as they arise in our lessons, is an ideal way to extend students' problem-solving repertoire (see Figure 6–3). While primary students may be able to solve the majority of problems using pictures, our goal is to help them develop other strategies so they will be better prepared to solve the more complex problems that will arise in the intermediate grades.

Communicating About the Strategy

Asking students to write about and talk about using tables is a great way to assess their understanding of this strategy. Try prompts like these:

- Describe the patterns you see on your table.

- What do the numbers in that row (or column) represent?

- Explain how making a table helped you find the answer.

- Explain how you know which number on the table is the answer to the problem.

- Explain how you know which two (or more) items in the problem should be used to create your table.

- Why was making a table a good strategy for solving this problem?

Figure 6–3 *This student shares her strategy for solving a class problem.*

A Note About Tables

Not all tables show patterns and functions. Some tables are simply data tables (e.g., a table showing the cost of refreshments at the movie theater or a table showing the number of points each player scored in a basketball game). Tables or charts can be used to record a variety of information and may not always show patterns. When we refer to making tables as a problem-solving strategy, however, we are generally referring to those tables that help us explore connected information through patterns as a way of getting to a problem solution. Helping students also see that other data might be recorded on a table, and that data from those tables might be used to solve problems, helps to build students' understanding of tables as a tool to solve problems. We may need to know how much each snack costs in order to solve a problem asking us to determine the cost for 3 of the snacks, but there is not a connection between the cost of popcorn and the cost of candy that would allow us to use patterns to complete that table. The data table simply provides us with the necessary information to solve the problem. Teachers might ask students to look at a table and determine if it has patterns or is simply a data table. Recognizing the difference between these types of tables will avoid misunderstandings for your students.

C L A S S R O O M - T E S T E D   T I P

Literature Link

Capitalize on students' interest in books by reading stories that provide the characters and situations for problem-solving activities. In Barbara deRubertis' *Count on Pablo,* Pablo helps his grandmother prepare to sell vegetables at the market, packaging them in sets (i.e., 2 onions, 5 peppers, 10 tomatoes), setting a context for the exploration of patterns and tables. Read the story to your students and have them create tables to show how many onions, peppers, or tomatoes would be in 1, 2, 3, 4, or 5 bags.

Questions for Discussion

1. How can attention to the Make a Table Strategy help your students learn to organize information? What can you do to ensure that your students recognize that the organization of data is a key for this strategy?

2. How might you simplify this strategy for students who are at a beginning level in their understanding?

3. How might you continue to challenge students who are successfully using tables as a problem-solving tool?

Strategy

Make an Organized List

Through group and classroom discussions, students can examine a variety of approaches and learn to evaluate appropriate strategies for a given solution.

—National Council of Teachers of Mathematics,
Curriculum and Evaluation Standards for School Mathematics

In the previous chapter, we discussed the importance of students organizing problem data to find a solution. While tables provide one way to organize data when there are connections between and among the data, this chapter will explore another way to organize data—the use of an organized list. Making an organized list is a valuable strategy when students are faced with problems that require determining all the possible combinations for a given situation. Students might be exploring all the possible drink/snack combinations that can be made from lemonade or milk, and cookies, brownies, or cupcakes. Students who are able to record and organize data in a systematic way are better able to keep track of the data and determine all of the possibilities.

Organize and Record

The two words describing this strategy—*organized list*—pinpoint the key ideas for the strategy.

1. *List* ideas, or get them out of your head and onto paper, so you will remember them.

2. Proceed in an *organized* way so you will know what has already been considered and can ensure that no possibilities have been missed.

Recording and organizing information are critical to effective problem solving and yet many students do not intuitively do either when they are faced with a problem. When attempting to figure out all the possible combinations of shirts (blue, red, and green) and pants (black and brown), students often randomly recite possibilities. As students proceed in a random fashion, they become confused and unsure of which combinations have already been given or which combinations have been missed altogether. Teaching students to find a starting point, to begin with one item and then exhaust all possible combinations with that item before moving on to another item, will help them proceed in an organized manner and recognize when they have listed all of the possibilities. And by recording each possibility, students simplify the task because they are able to keep track of their ideas and double-check their thinking.

blue shirt—black pants
blue shirt—brown pants

Those are the only pants, so I'm done with the blue shirt. I'll try the red shirt next.

red shirt—black pants
red shirt—brown pants

Now I'm done with the red shirt. I'll try the green shirt.

green shirt—black pants
green shirt—brown pants

I have no more shirts, so I must be done!

 Hands-on introductory activities help students experiment with this strategy. In early experiences, students might use shirt and pant cutouts (see the template on the CD) to represent various shirt or pant color combinations, trying the different combinations and then recording each one. Or students might use color tiles to represent each color of shirt and pants. While students try the different combinations with hands-on materials, encourage them to find an organized way of proceeding and to record the combinations they have tried. Young students might record by simply coloring each shirt and pants possibility, while older students might make a list to record each combination. Have your students share their approaches with one another and discuss the different ways in which they chose to record their combinations.

Laying the Foundation for More Sophisticated Skills

Organized list problems can begin quite simply. In simple combination problems, a goal is to help students understand the importance of finding a starting point and exhausting all possibilities before moving on. Consider the following problem:

Chris wanted a snack after school. She could have raisins or pretzels to eat. She could have orange juice, milk, or water to drink. If Chris could pick one thing to eat and one thing to drink, what are the different possibilities for her after-school snack?

First-grade students attempted to solve this problem. Amber said, "She could have pretzels and milk, and she could have raisins and orange juice." Amber continued to state possibilities with no organized approach. Amber found five different combinations and stopped. Stevie said, "I just did raisins with orange juice, and raisins with milk, and raisins with water. Then I did pretzels with orange juice and pretzels with milk and pretzels with water. It's just 3 ways with each." Stevie knew that he got all of the possibilities because he did it in an organized way. Stevie's choice of beginning with raisins was a good one, since it is the first snack mentioned, but even if he had started with pretzels, as long as he moved in an organized manner he could keep track of what had already been done, and would have been able to find the solution.

Once students have internalized the skill of moving through data in an organized way, helping them refine the ways in which they record their ideas will help them further develop their skills. Students begin to recognize that using initials or symbols might be more efficient than writing entire words on a list and so raisins becomes *r*, and pretzels becomes *p*. As the complexity of problems increases, our students benefit from the foundational skills they have developed through their experiences with simpler problems.

CLASSROOM-TESTED TIP

Introducing Organized Lists

Give students a worksheet with three cups and two circles (see the drinks and cookies manipulatives template on the CD). Ask them to color the cups red, yellow, and orange to represent fruit punch, lemonade, and orange drink. Ask them to color the circles brown and yellow to represent chocolate and sugar cookies. Have students cut out the cups and cookies. Ask the students how many drink/cookie combinations are possible. Allow them to experiment with the drink and cookie cutouts, and then ask some students to share their answers. (There will probably be a variety of answers!) Tell students you are going to explore the problem together. Be sure to record each combination as you demonstrate it for the class. Show students how to begin with one item, such as fruit punch, and determine all the combinations for that item before moving on.

Fruit punch and chocolate cookie
Fruit punch and sugar cookie

Ask students, "Are there any other combinations that you can make with fruit punch?" Students should be able to tell you without a doubt that there are no more, since you've used both kinds of cookies. Move on to lemonade and follow the same process. When you are finished, ask students if they are sure you named all of the possibilities. They should feel confident that no combination has been missed. When you ask students to make lists to solve problems, try to give purpose to the activity by asking students to circle their preference after finding all of the possibilities. Asking "Which drink/cookie combination would you choose?" will provide a reason for having to figure out all of those possibilities.

Note: If students are unable to write lists, provide them with a template to record the possibilities by coloring (see template on CD) or ask them to draw the possibilities.

Combinations Versus Permutations

The previous snack problem is an example of a combination problem. In combination problems, the order does not matter. Having a snack of raisins and water is the same as a snack of water and raisins. They are not two different snack choices. The organized list strategy also supports students with permutation problems. In permutation problems, order matters. If there are three cars in a race (a blue car, a green car, and a red car) and we want to figure out all of the different orders in which the cars might finish the race, we find the blue car could finish first, the green car could finish second, and the red car could finish third. Even though it is the same three cars, a different possibility would be the blue car finishing first, the red car finishing second, and the green car finishing third. While these problems are a bit different from combination problems, the organized list strategy supports students as they simplify the somewhat confusing task. Again, beginning with one car and exhausting all of the possibilities with that car finishing first, then moving to the next car, would be a good plan to stay on track.

> blue car, green car, red car
> blue car, red car, green car
> *There are no other ways to do it with the blue car finishing first. So what if the green car finished first?*

> green car, red car, blue car
> green car, blue car, red car
> *Now, we're done with options for the green car finishing first, so what if the red car finished first?*

> red car, blue car, green car
> red car, green car, blue car
> *There are no more cars, so those must be the only ways the cars can finish the race!*

CLASSROOM-TESTED TIP

Demonstrating the Need for Organization

Try a demonstration with three students in your class. Ask them to get in a line to sharpen their pencils. Create the line in front of the class—for example, Megan, then Colleen, then Erica. Ask the class how many other ways they might line up. As students in the class suggest other ways in which to order the three students, switch their order in the line. After a while, ask students, "Is that all the possible ways? How many ways were there? Are you sure we've tried them all? Are you sure we haven't repeated any?" Ask students to talk with a partner and see if they can figure out a way to be sure that all the possible orders have been tried without repeating any. You might prompt them with questions such as "How many ways can they line up if Megan is first? If Colleen is first? If Erica is first?" Students may come up with the idea of writing down each possibility, or they may even come up with an organized method to be sure they don't miss any possibilities (i.e., beginning with all of the possibilities in which Megan is first and then moving to Colleen being first in line). Praise their logical thinking as they share their ideas. Begin again, this time keeping an organized list.

Formulas and Organized Lists

As students work on organized lists, they develop the groundwork for discovering mathematical formulas that may help them arrive at answers when the data become more challenging in the intermediate grades. Consider the problem in which students need to determine the number of shirt/pants combinations possible with 2 shirts (blue and green) and 3 pants (red, yellow, and black). As students work on similar combination problems, they may begin to notice a formula—if there are x of one item and y of another item, then there are $x \times y$ possibilities. Students will discover that 2 shirts and 3 pants will yield 2×3 or 6 possible combinations. While this is a helpful insight for intermediate students who are beginning to encounter problems with more sophisticated data, it is important that our students discover and understand formulas rather than being told to memorize the formula. By simply memorizing a formula, students are missing out on the development of organized thinking and lack the understanding to know why they are performing the calculations. Both organized thinking and the use of formulas help our students solve problems. Students who have facility with both are more likely to find solutions to the varied problems they might face.

A Look at Student Work

Primary students begin by experimenting with actual objects or manipulatives. Students may simply be asked to color pictures to record and remember their combinations (e.g., see the cookie and drink recording sheet on the CD). Once the concept of combinations has been explored in a concrete way, students may begin to draw objects rather than use the actual items (see Figure 7–1). This student drew the possible valentines and then added to find the number of possibilities.

Students may begin lists by recording the entire word, but soon see that initials or abbreviations work well and save time (see Figure 7–2). Share the varied ways that students represent items on their lists. It is the organization of the items that is most important, not the words or initials that are selected to represent those items. This second grader used a systematic approach to listing the possible snack and drink combinations, beginning with the possibilities that included milk and then listing the combinations that included lemonade.

The writing in Figure 7–3 illustrates this student's thinking. She explains what she did so she would not get confused, explaining that she crossed out the words (apple pie, pumpkin pie, and cherry pie) as she listed each type of pie, and that writing down the possibilities helped her. Insights about how students approach a problem-solving task are invaluable.

Many primary problems are easy to solve, and even without an organized list, students could find the correct answer. It is important to remember, however, that our goal is to build students' problem-solving skills, so they will be able to solve in-

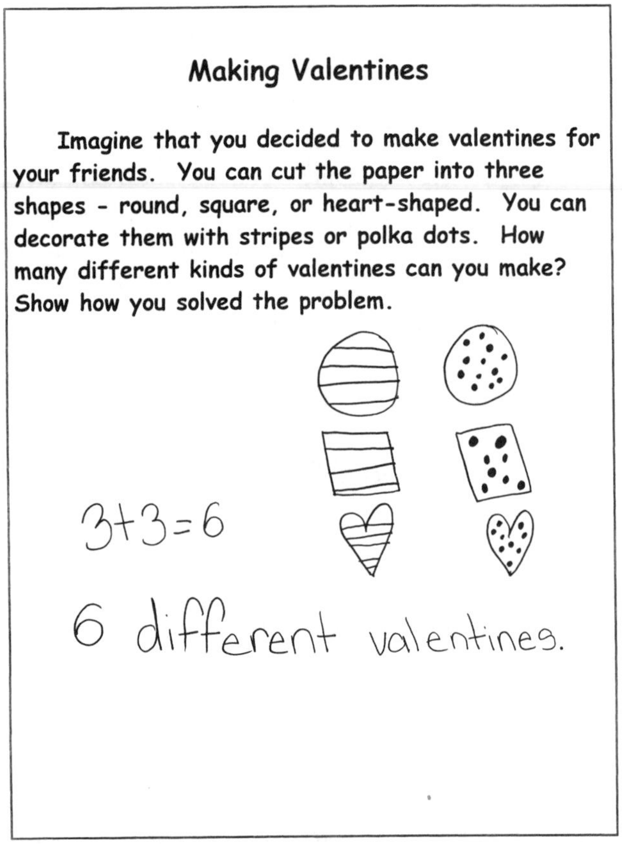

Making Valentines

Imagine that you decided to make valentines for your friends. You can cut the paper into three shapes - round, square, or heart-shaped. You can decorate them with stripes or polka dots. How many different kinds of valentines can you make? Show how you solved the problem.

$3+3=6$

6 different valentines.

Figure 7–1 *This student draws each possible valentine.*

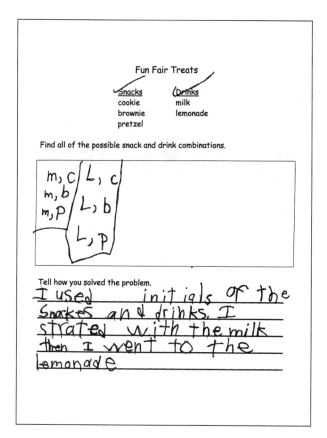

Figure 7–2 *This student used initials to represent each item and moved through the data in a systematic way.*

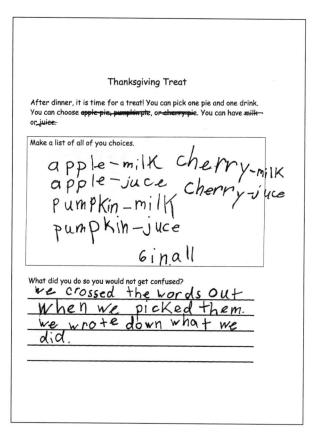

Figure 7–3 *This student explains how she simplified the task.*

creasingly difficult problems. The correct answer is not our sole concern. In fact, it will not matter next month or next year that our students got the right answer on today's simple problem, but it will matter that they developed the skills related to the *organized list* strategy. Helping students learn to organize their thinking, progress through the problem in a systematic way, and find ways to record their ideas so they will remember what has been done, are all critical components of this strategy.

Communicating About the Strategy

Don't forget to have students write about and talk about their strategy for solving the problem. Try prompts like these:

- Where will you get started? What will you do next?

- What does it mean to be organized?

- Why is it important to be organized when making your list?

- Why is it important to record your combinations?

75

▧ How will you record your data?

▧ Are you sure there are no other possible combinations? Why?

▧ Why was making an organized list a good strategy for solving this problem?

CLASSROOM-TESTED TIP

Problem-Solving Centers

Centers provide students with repeated practice in problem solving. Centers might simply pose a daily problem, with solutions available in an envelope at the center for students to check their work, or they might present problems for student pairs to discuss and solve. For a more exciting variation, you might post a Problem-of-the-Week (P.O.W.) challenge each Monday, with students placing their solutions (and explanations for students able to write about their thinking) in an envelope at the center once they have solved the problem. On Friday of each week, the teacher randomly selects one, or more, solutions from the envelope for review. A right answer and explanation earns the student a place on a *POWerful Problem Solvers* poster for the coming week!

Questions for Discussion

1. Why is it important for teachers to think aloud while demonstrating this problem-solving strategy?

2. What are *combinations*? What are *permutations*? How are they alike and different?

3. How does using lists help students make complicated problems simpler? Is helping students find a way to make hard problems easier a goal of problem-solving instruction? Why?

Strategy

Draw a Picture or Diagram

The act of representing encourages children to focus on the essential characteristics of a situation.

—National Council of Teachers of Mathematics,
Curriculum and Evaluation Standards for School Mathematics

The old adage, "A picture is worth a thousand words," can be true in problem solving. Drawing a picture or diagram helps students visualize the problem. In problem solving, we encourage students to get problems out of their heads, to make them visual. For primary students, we begin by acting out problem situations as we add real candy to a dish and then transition to the use of manipulatives (e.g., cubes or counters) to represent the candy. Then we help students create their own visuals by drawing pictures or diagrams to represent the candy in order to see and solve the problem. By drawing pictures to represent the data, problems that initially appear complex become easy to solve.

Using Pictures to Solve Problems

Very young students have difficulty solving problems in the abstract and rely on pictures to allow them to see the problem situation. With the help of pictures, students become able to find solutions to problems that are otherwise confusing to them. Consider this simple problem:

There are 3 horses. How many legs are there?

Young students may recognize that a horse has 4 legs, but they are unable to mentally calculate the number of legs on 3 horses. By drawing simple pictures of the horses, students are able to visualize the data and then count the legs they have drawn to find the answer. The picture provides them with a path for getting to the solution.

Students are beginning to learn the operations of addition and subtraction in the primary grades, but even before they are able to apply that understanding to build addition or subtraction equations to solve problems, their ability to draw pictures allows them to solve many math problems. Consider the following problem:

10 ghosts were in the haunted house. 3 more ghosts flew in the window. How many ghosts were in the haunted house?

Students who begin with an understanding of combining or joining two groups (the ghosts in the haunted house and the ghosts who flew in the window) are able to draw and count all of the ghosts to find the correct solution. These young students are demonstrating an understanding of the concept of addition (joining groups) as they draw the pictures. As their understanding of addition is refined, their drawings will be replaced with simple addition equations.

Even as problems gain complexity, pictures provide students with a means to find solutions, as in the following problem.

There were 4 plates on the table. There were 3 cookies on each plate. How many cookies were on the table?

While some students might solve the problem using addition ($3 + 3 + 3 + 3$) or even multiplication (4×3), primary students can draw pictures to find the solution. While the problem data may be difficult for some students to process in their heads, a simple diagram of the plates allows them to see the cookies on each plate and count them to reveal the total number of cookies. The problem is immediately simplified by creating a picture of the data.

New Meaning for the Word Picture

Before they are able to write words to express their ideas, primary students share their ideas through pictures. Prekindergarteners draw very simplistic pictures (e.g., a person as a circle head with stick arms and legs) and so we encourage them to add detail and color to their drawings. But in math, drawings serve a different purpose. Drawings are ways our students get math ideas onto paper so they can better see the ideas, process those ideas, and solve problems based on them. For young students, the pictures may be their sole way of communicating their ideas, but as students begin to develop written language skills, it is important to help them transition to diagrams that represent ideas (e.g., a square to represent a table rather than a more realistic table with 4 legs). Coloring the picture becomes unnecessary unless the colors represent problem data. As students begin to mature and understand that pictures are representations of math ideas, take the time to help them understand what is important when drawing pictures to solve problems. Dogs do not have to have ears and eyes and noses. Perhaps a circle or a tally mark might even represent a dog. Some students often spend so much time creating a detailed picture that they never end up solving the problem. Focus students on the use of pictures as a part of the problem-solving process.

CLASSROOM-TESTED TIP

Sharing Drawings at Circle Time

It is important for primary students to begin to see ways to represent ideas without lots of detail in their pictures. After posing a problem in which students draw the data, have students share the different ways in which they represented the data. Sharing at circle time is a great way to do this. During circle time, students sit in a circle so that each student is facing the others and can see and hear what they are sharing. Have some students stand and show their drawings, prompting them to tell how they represented the data. While one child may have drawn cats and turtles, another used circles to represent the animals, and still another used x's. Praise students for finding ways to show 2 cats without drawing 2 cats. Ask probing questions like "Did you need to draw it to look like a cat?" or "Could we still count how many animals were in the park with these circles?" Display their drawings on bulletin boards or show samples using an overhead projector or video visualizer. Providing opportunities for students to reflect on how they represent the problem data and allowing them to see each other's representations will help transition them from elaborate drawings. Students will move toward more abstract forms of representation at different rates, but our goal is to gently push them to use diagrams in the most effective way.

Simplifying Through Pictures

Problems can be confusing when several pieces of data are presented within the problem. Drawing a diagram helps to clarify the problem situation and allows students to think about the data one piece at a time. Consider the following problem:

> There were 3 flowers in the garden. The yellow flower was taller than the red flower. The pink flower was shorter than the red flower. Which flower was tallest?

By simply moving step by step and recording each color of flower, students can proceed through the problem with ease.

First fact: **The yellow flower was taller than the red flower.**

This fact is represented by drawing a tall yellow flower and a shorter red flower.

Second fact: **The pink flower was shorter than the red flower.**

Now students draw a pink flower that is shorter than the red one.

With the diagram complete, not only can students clearly see the size of the flowers, but there is a sense of accomplishment in solving this initially confusing problem. The problem was confusing until it became visual through the act of drawing a picture. The problem got easier because students could see the data.

Initially, primary students draw pictures to see very simple data, but by second grade, the data become more complex. Again, pictures can help simplify it.

> **There were 16 children at the birthday party. Each child could choose the color of treat bag that they would like to take home. Half of the children chose a red bag. Four children chose a blue bag. The rest chose a yellow treat bag. How many children chose a yellow treat bag?**

The ability to draw the treat bags, and then decide what half might be, supports students in finding this solution. Along with helping students visualize the problem data, the act of drawing pictures assists students who might be intimidated by the seemingly difficult problem. Our goal will always be to help students discover the most efficient way to solve a problem (e.g., possibly creating equations to find the number of each color of treat bag), but we recognize the importance of helping our students develop a repertoire of strategies to find solutions. There may be times when drawing pictures is the most efficient, or the most understandable, method for finding a solution. Discussing the varied ways to get to the solution is an important component of the problem-solving experience.

CLASSROOM-TESTED TIP

The Value of Modeling and Discussions

At times it becomes obvious that simplifying problems with pictures or diagrams may not be intuitive for all students. We may notice that some students become frustrated when we pose problems that appear confusing. It may be helpful to do some modeling for our students, sharing our thinking, asking questions, and supporting them as we explore a problem together. Below is an example of how to do this.

> **There are 12 flowers in the garden. Three of the flowers are red. Two flowers are pink. The rest are yellow. How many yellow flowers are in the garden?**

While some students may immediately see that drawing a diagram is a way to simplify this problem, others may be confused by the data. Support students by exploring the problem together. Ask them if seeing a picture of the problem might help them find the answer. Have them draw a picture to represent the 12 flowers. Rather than drawing detailed flowers, ask them if there are other easier ways to represent the flowers. They might suggest simple flowers (e.g., no stem or leaves) or circles to represent the flowers. Ask students to select a way and draw 12 of them—one for each flower in the garden. Demonstrate for them on the chalkboard or overhead projector. Read the first part of the problem together and ask the students to circle the red flowers. Label that section on your model "red," or color the drawings red, and "think aloud" that your label or coloring will help you remember why you circled them. Read the next part of the problem and ask them to circle the pink flowers. Ask students how you might remember what you have done (e.g., label them or color them). Read the last part of the problem. Ask students to circle the remaining flowers. Ask them how they will know how many flowers are yellow (e.g., count them). Reread the problem. Ask the students to use their pictures to tell you how many yellow flowers are in the garden. Ask students to talk about what was easy or hard about the problem and how the picture helped them solve it.

Differentiating Instruction in Problem Solving

Often within the same classroom, students are at a variety of levels in their understanding and use of a particular problem-solving strategy. Differentiating a problem for varied groups within the classroom allows us to explore a strategy with all students while offering appropriate variations of the problem to meet our students' varied ability levels. A teacher might pose the following problem to students as they explore drawing pictures to solve problems:

> **Julie is having a Valentine's Day party. Her mother bought 2 pizzas to serve to the party guests. Each pizza had 8 slices. How many slices of pizza did they have for their party?**

While the problem is appropriate for many students within the class, others will benefit from a more-challenging variation of the problem.

Julie is having a Valentine's Day party. Her mother bought 2 large pizzas and 2 medium pizzas to serve to the party guests. Each large pizza had 8 slices and each medium pizza had 6 slices. How many slices of pizza did they have for their party?

While both problems can be solved by drawing pictures, the second problem requires students to consider more complex data (e.g., 2 different sizes of pizza). Even though some students may be working on a slightly different problem, the teacher is able to facilitate whole-class discussions about the use of pictures to solve problems. In both cases, students can talk about why they chose the strategy to get them to the solution, discuss ways in which they can draw the pizzas, represent the slices on each pizza, and count or add to find the solution. And for students who might quickly complete the task, the teacher can offer the following challenge:

If each person at the party got 2 slices of pizza, how many people were at the party?

Through this additional question, a small group of students can be challenged to use their data from the original problem, and their understanding of pairs or fair sharing, to determine how many people were at the party. Again, a picture (e.g., circling or marking every two pieces of pizza) is a possible strategy for finding the solution. Adding layers of complexity to problems for specific students will keep them engaged and continue to push the development of their thinking skills. (See the *challenge* activities on many of the CD student activities.)

Working in groups or with partners has many benefits in problem-solving instruction. It allows students to share ideas and hear each other's thinking. But students often work at different speeds, with some groups finishing while others are still actively engaged with the task. Teachers might consider posing a problem to all groups and asking groups to raise their hands as they finish the task. The teacher can then move to that pair or group and ask them to explain or justify their answer in order to check their understanding. If students are ready to move on, the teacher might then pose a challenge problem to keep them involved in the activity.

CLASSROOM-TESTED TIP

Manipulative Baskets

Many students find problem solving easier when they can see or act out a problem. Have manipulative baskets readily available for students during problem-solving experiences. Manipulative baskets provide students with tools to see and experience the problems. Baskets might include counters, cubes, paper cutouts, or other materials that support students in solving the problem. Baskets might be placed at each table, or in a central location, so students can choose to use the manipulatives when they need support in *seeing* the problem.

A Look at Student Work

For very young students, drawing pictures is an aid for understanding the simplest math concepts. As students are posed problems in which they must add 2 happy pumpkins and 3 scary pumpkins, they simply draw pictures of the happy and scary pumpkins. This enables them to count their pictures to find the total number of pumpkins. The picture helps to make the problem real and understandable. The student work in Figure 8–1 demonstrates how pictures supported a kindergarten student in solving a problem. Students were told that there were 7 friends and 5 pens and asked if every friend would get a pen. This student simply drew the friends and the pens and

There are 5 pens and 7 friends. She needs 2 more pens.

Figure 8–1 *The answer to the problem becomes clear after the student draws the problem data.*

saw the difference between the groups. She dictated her answer to the teacher, who recorded it on her paper.

In Figure 8–2, a first-grade student was able to find the solution to the problem through a simple diagram. Her writing shows her recognition of how drawing pictures can simplify a math task as she remarks that "Drawing a picture helps you because you can see it on your paper and count it easily."

Some primary students spend time making more realistic pictures than are necessary to solve math problems. The student in Figure 8–3 is trying to determine how many apples are in 5 bags if there are 5 apples in each bag. The drawing includes unnecessary details, took an extensive amount of time to complete, and resulted in an incorrect answer. More time was spent on the drawing than on ensuring that the data were accurate. Having students share alternate ways to represent data (e.g., simple circles or x's) will help students see what is important when drawing pictures as a problem-solving strategy

Students are often quick to answer problems before fully investigating the data. A picture can help students recognize errors in their thinking. In the problem in Figure 8–4, the student first decides that the sandwich can be split into four pieces by making 4 "cuts", but after making 3 "cuts" she recognizes the error in her thinking. Her writing indicates that drawing a picture alerted her to her error. For all students, a picture or diagram can be a great way to check for errors in thinking.

For some students, drawing pictures or diagrams is a way to get jump-started when they are having a hard time understanding or visualizing a problem. Drawing a diagram of the seating arrangement in Figure 8–5 helped the student get started, but once he visualized the seating arrangement, he was able to use equations to find the solution.

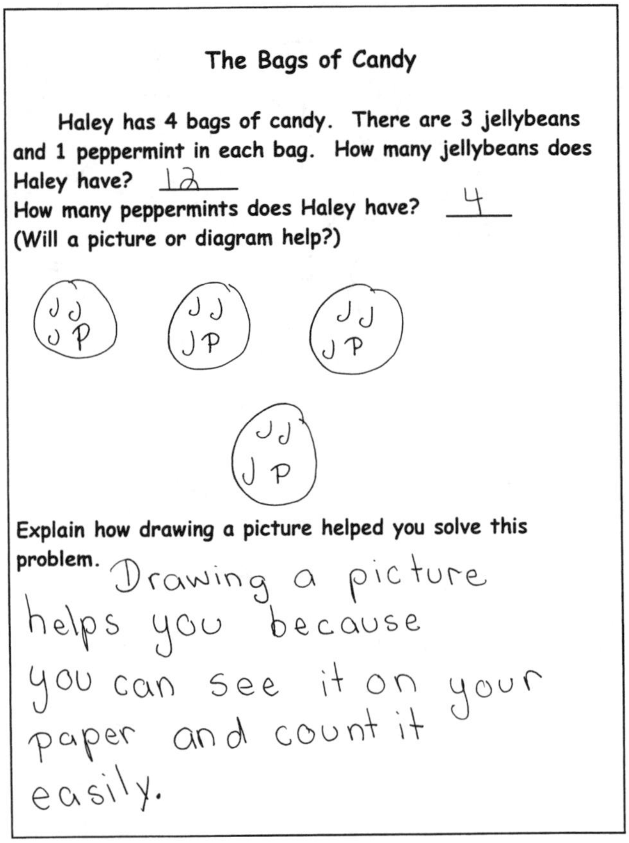

The Bags of Candy

Haley has 4 bags of candy. There are 3 jellybeans and 1 peppermint in each bag. How many jellybeans does Haley have? __12__

How many peppermints does Haley have? __4__

(Will a picture or diagram help?)

Explain how drawing a picture helped you solve this problem. Drawing a picture helps you because you can see it on your paper and count it easily.

Figure 8–2 *This student's simple diagram helped her find a solution.*

Figure 8–3 *The level of detail in this student's drawing is not necessary for solving the problem.*

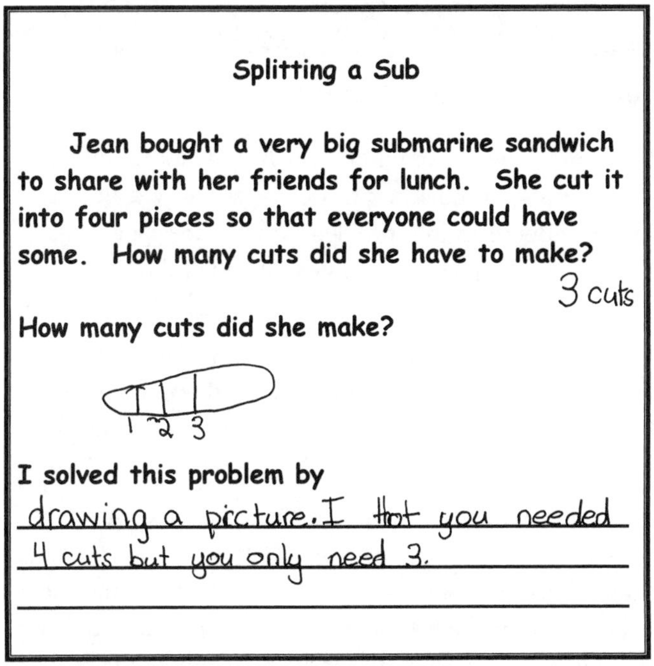

Splitting a Sub

Jean bought a very big submarine sandwich to share with her friends for lunch. She cut it into four pieces so that everyone could have some. How many cuts did she have to make?

3 cuts

How many cuts did she make?

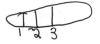

I solved this problem by

drawing a picture. I thot you needed 4 cuts but you only need 3.

Figure 8-4 *This student began to draw "cuts" in her diagram expecting to draw 4 "cuts." Her drawing helped her recognize the error in her initial thinking.*

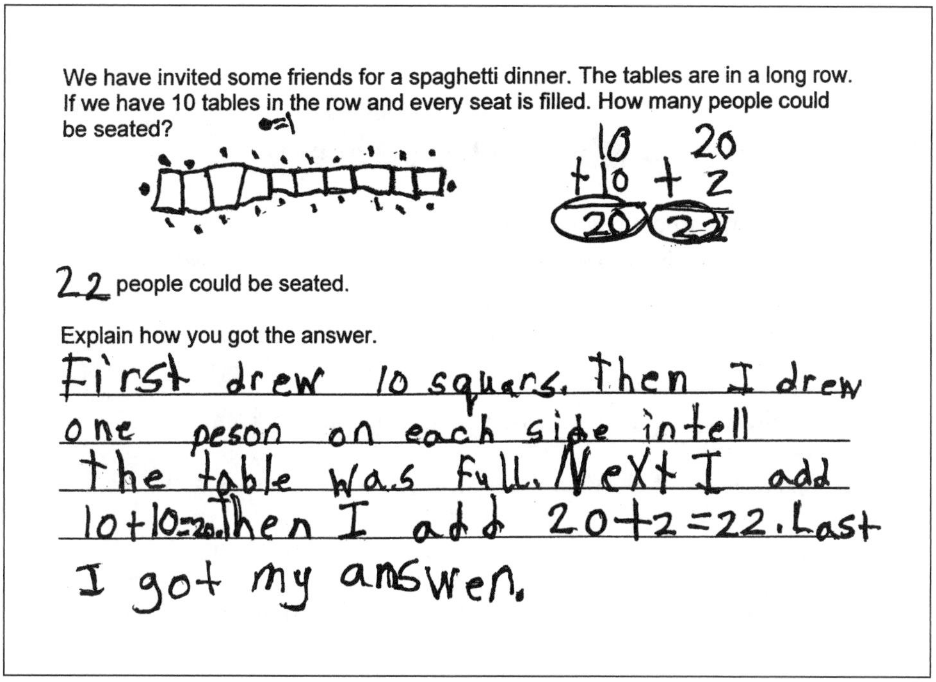

We have invited some friends for a spaghetti dinner. The tables are in a long row. If we have 10 tables in the row and every seat is filled. How many people could be seated?

$$10 \quad 20$$
$$+10 \quad +2$$
$$\overline{20} \quad \overline{22}$$

22 people could be seated.

Explain how you got the answer.

First drew 10 squars. then I drew one peson on each side intell the table was full. Next I add 10+10=20 then I add 20+2=22. Last I got my answer.

Figure 8-5 *This student began by drawing a picture to visualize the problem, but was then able to use addition to solve the problem.*

CLASSROOM-TESTED TIP

Using Manipulatives to Visualize a Problem

Many problems that sound confusing are simplified when students are able to visualize the problem. The use of manipulatives is a great way to engage students in problem solving and show them that problems often appear more difficult than they actually are. Begin by posing a problem like the following:

Pat stacked 4 boxes on his desk. The yellow box was below the green box. The red box was above the green box. The blue box was between the red and green boxes. What was the order of the boxes from top to bottom?

Provide each pair of students with a yellow, green, blue, and red connecting cube and ask them to stack their cubes in the order that Pat stacked his boxes. Read the clues one at a time. Encourage students to talk with their partners as they create their stacks. Look around the room at the stacks of cubes to see which pairs may need help. Once students have the answer, talk about the problem. Was it easier than they thought it would be? What made it easier? If they didn't have the blocks, how might they make it easier? The manipulatives allow students to do the problem one clue at a time, to simply move colors above, below, or in-between as needed, and provides a way of recording or remembering what has been done. Once students' anxiety is lower, transition them into using paper-and-pencil sketches to do similar problems. Building skills and alleviating anxiety work hand-in-hand to create better problem solvers!

Communicating About the Strategy

Don't forget to have students write and talk about their strategies. For very young students, we might ask them to tell us about their thinking and we would record their words on the paper for them. As students are able to write on their own, encourage them to write about their thinking (see Figure 8–6). Try prompts like these:

- Why was drawing a picture a good way to solve this problem?

- Does a picture need to be detailed to help you solve a problem? Why?

- Can a picture or diagram help you find mistakes in your work? How?

- How did a picture help you better understand this problem?

Figure 8–6 *Writing about their problem solving challenges students to think about
what they have done.*

Questions for Discussion

1. How can the use of pictures and diagrams simplify difficult tasks?

2. Pictures and diagrams help students visualize problems. How is the use of manipulatives similar to using pictures and diagrams? How is it different? How is acting out a problem situation similar to using pictures and diagrams? How is it different?

3. How might teachers help students see a variety of ways to picture or diagram a problem?

4. How might teachers challenge different levels of students in the same classroom?

CHAPTER 9

Strategy

Guess, Check, and Revise

*When problem solving becomes an integral part of classroom instruction
and children experience success in solving problems, they gain confidence
in doing mathematics and develop persevering and inquiring minds.*

—National Council of Teachers of Mathematics,
Curriculum and Evaluation Standards for School Mathematics

The Guess, Check, and Revise strategy begins with a guess. The guess provides students with a way of getting started on the problem. The guess, however, is only the beginning of the process. After plugging the guess into the problem situation, students must use their reasoning and number sense skills to adjust the guess until the correct answer is found. The Guess, Check, and Revise strategy allows students to dive in and try an answer and then challenges them to use their understanding of numbers and operations to adjust that answer until it is correct.

Beginning with a Guess

Often students are faced with a problem in which they don't know how to begin. Students might be shown five clear sandwich bags, each containing a different number of snap cubes (e.g., 1, 2, 3, 4, or 5 cubes). The teacher might pose the problem:

> We need 12 cubes to build a tower. Can we choose 3 bags and get exactly 12 cubes? Which 3 bags should we choose?

This problem may be frustrating for some students. How could they be expected to know which bags to choose? Rather than leaving them feeling confused, Guess,

Check, and Revise thinking encourages them to jump in and try it! We encourage students to select 3 bags and see how many cubes they have in those bags. If Kara picked the bags with 1, 2, and 3 cubes, she could simply count to find out that she had 6 total cubes. While that is not the correct answer, her wrong choices provide her with important information on what she might try next. "It's not enough!" Kara said. "I need more cubes in the bags." Kara's next guess was bags with 2, 4, and 5 cubes in them. She counted to find that she had 11 cubes. "It's still not enough." she said. "I need some bags with more." Next, Kara picked the bags with 3, 4, and 5 cubes in them and counted to find 12 total cubes. "I knew it!" she said. After each bag selection and cube count, Kara's understanding of numbers guided her to revise which bags she chose.

At lower primary levels, any guess is a good way to jump-start students' thinking, but our next goal is to help students begin with a reasonable guess—to show them how to use their number sense and estimation skills to begin with a guess that is "in the ballpark." Discuss initial guesses with students. Together, look for clues in the problem that will help them make educated guesses that will lessen the number of revisions they will have to make. Consider the following problem:

> **Allison had pennies, nickels, and dimes in her piggy bank. She shook it and 3 coins fell out. Her coins were worth 16 cents. Which coins did she have?**

Students should not be starting with a guess of 3 pennies. It would not be reasonable, considering she had a total of 16 cents. And students should not be starting with a guess of 3 dimes. Again, it would not be reasonable because 2 dimes is more than 16 cents. Practicing just the first step of this problem-solving strategy will help students better understand a reasonable first guess. Pose simple problems and ask students to whisper their estimate (guess) to a partner. Have students share their guesses, and how they came up with those guesses, with the class. Logical reasoning and number sense play an important role in this strategy.

Revising the Guess

Revision is a critical step in this strategy. It is unlikely that students will guess the correct answer on the first try, so they must then plug their guesses into the problem and adjust the initial guess until they've found the correct answer. Students will need to recognize when their guess is too large or too small and will need to be able to make adjustments until the answer is found. Let's consider the coin problem again. If Allison had pennies, nickels, and dimes in her piggy bank and she shook it and 3 coins fell out that were worth 16 cents, students might use guess, check, and revise thinking to move toward a solution.

"I think she had a dime and 2 nickels."

That would be a total of 20 cents, which is too much. The guess was a reasonable one in that it wasn't way too low (e.g., 3 pennies) or way too high (e.g., 3 dimes), but it did not prove to be the correct answer. An adjustment was needed.

"That was too much. Maybe she had a dime and 2 pennies."

The student realized he needed to choose coins with lesser values, but now his answer is too low.

"That's not enough, it's just 12 cents. I can try a dime and a nickel and a penny. That's it! It's 16 cents!"

It took several revisions before the student arrived at the correct answer, but the revisions were thoughtful ones. He was using the data he observed to make each new adjustment. Practice with this type of thinking will help primary students develop their number sense as well as their observation skills. When evaluating student work, look for evidence that each revision led the student closer to the answer.

Thinking aloud is especially important when demonstrating this strategy. Both in selecting a first guess and in revising guesses throughout the process, it is important that students understand the thinking involved in each step. Students need to know that when you are not sure how to begin, you might just try a guess to get you started. Students need to hear your thought processes as you adjust and readjust your answers. Students need to know it's okay not to get the answer on the first guess. Students benefit from hearing our thinking and from questions that challenge them to reflect on how to solve problems. Try comments and questions such as "This problem looks confusing. Do you think if I try something I might be able to figure it out?" or "What could we try?" Class discussions prior to starting on a problem give students a chance to process the task and consider possible methods for approaching the problem.

CLASSROOM-TESTED TIP

Introducing Guess, Check, and Revise Thinking

Draw cookies or glue cookie cutouts (see template on CD) to 5 paper plates. Glue 1 cookie on one plate, 2 cookies on another plate, 3 cookies on a plate, 4 cookies on a plate, and 5 cookies on a plate. Tape the plates to the board so all students can see them. Tell the students that you picked two of the plates and that you ate all of the cookies on the two plates. Altogether you ate 5 cookies. They will need to figure out which two plates of cookies you picked. Have a student guess two plates. Together, by counting, figure out how many cookies were on those two plates. Ask the students to tell you if these two plates had too many, too few, or just the right amount of cookies. If the guess was not correct, tell the students that they will need to try again. Ask for another guess, but this time ask them to use what they now know to get closer to the answer. After the revised guess, ask students, "Did we pick too many, too few, or just the right amount of cookies?" Students may be asked to respond with thumbs up (too high), thumbs down (too low), or a flat hand parallel to the ground (just right). Continue until you've found an answer. Try a few more, with students working in pairs or groups to allow them to discuss their guesses and revisions. Praise students for reasonable guesses and thoughtful revisions.

Variation: Challenge students to select 3 plates that have a given amount of cookies on them.

Using Guess, Check, and Revise with Equations

A student might look at the following missing addend equation and not know where to begin.

_____ + 9 = 27

This is when students often put their heads down in frustration because they don't know how to get started. The Guess, Check, and Revise strategy provides them with a starting point so they can find a way to get to a correct answer. One way to find an answer could be to try a number in the blank—for example, 16.

<u>16</u> + 9 = 27?
 "16 + 9 = 25. That addend is too small. We need a larger one. Let's try 19."
<u>19</u> + 9 = 27?
 "That's still not right. 19+ 9 = 28. Now our sum is too large. The addend has to be greater than 16, but less than 19. Let's try 18."
18 + 9 = 27?
 "It worked! 18 is the correct answer."

Without knowing how to begin, the student was able to find the correct answer by using the Guess, Check, and Revise method. While other students may find the answer in other ways (e.g., using inverse operations), our goal is to arm students with varied ways to find solutions and enhance their repertoire of strategies so they have options as they attempt the varied problems they face. Ultimately, our goal is for students to solve problems in the most efficient way possible, but the ability to guess, check, and revise to find an answer will offer a starting point for students who might otherwise be overwhelmed with the task. And the strong emphasis on starting with a reasonable answer and observing data in order to revise and adjust it provides invaluable lessons for all students.

Understanding the Role of Positive Attitudes

This strategy depends on the development of positive problem-solving attitudes, as we discussed in the Introduction. Students must be risk takers and be willing to jump in, even when they are unsure how to begin. Students are sometimes hesitant to guess an answer for fear that it will be wrong. Assure them that it is a fine way to begin a problem—as long as they check their guess and adjust it as needed. Allowing them to work with partners and take risks together will help them build their confidence (see Figure 9–1). Students must also be patient and persistent as they check and revise each guess. Each guess should bring them closer to the correct answer.

CLASSROOM-TESTED TIP

Find the Addends

Give students quick and repeated practice with guess-and-check thinking, as well as practice with addition, by posing simple number problems for the class to solve and discuss. Write a number on the board (e.g., 21) and tell students that it is the sum of 3 addends. Write 5 possible addends on the board (e.g., 3, 5, 7, 9, 11) and ask students to work with a partner to find the 3 addends that work. Walk through the room to listen to their initial guesses and adjustments. As students share their answers, be sure to have them talk about their thinking. What was their initial guess? How did they revise it? And remember, there may be more than one possible answer (e.g., $3 + 7 + 11 = 21$ and $5 + 7 + 9 = 21$). There also may be other methods for finding the addends! Some students may begin by subtracting an addend from the sum (e.g., $21 - 11 = 10$) and then finding a pair of addends that equal 10. We strive to develop the critical thinking skills related to the guess-and-check strategy, but we also recognize that there are other ways to find solutions.

Figure 9–1 *Students are more willing to take risks when they have the support of a partner.*

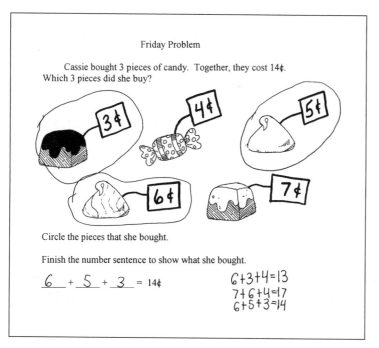

Friday Problem

Cassie bought 3 pieces of candy. Together, they cost 14¢.
Which 3 pieces did she buy?

Circle the pieces that she bought.

Finish the number sentence to show what she bought.

_6_ + _5_ + _3_ = 14¢

6+3+4=13
7+6+4=17
6+5+3=14

Figure 9–2 *A look at this student's guesses shows thoughtful
revisions that led to a correct answer.*

A Look at Student Work

Guess-and-check thinking provides students with a way of getting started on problems and then helps them adjust their thinking to ultimately get to a solution. As you
can see from the number sentences on the side of the student's paper in Figure 9–2,
the child made several attempts before he found a workable solution. It is evident
from his trials that he did a good job adjusting his thinking. When his first guess was
too low, he chose larger numbers on his second try. When those numbers were too
large, he adjusted them down to find the correct answer.

In Figure 9–3, the student's work and explanation show her realization that her
first guess was too high and show a reasonable adjustment using lower numbers. In
Figure 9–4, the student made three attempts before arriving at the correct answer,
but each attempt brought her closer to the answer. *Tip:* Asking students to number
their trials will help you assess whether their revisions are thoughtful ones as it will
allow you to track the order of their trials.

Communicating About the Strategy

In order to continue to develop students' understanding, don't forget to have students talk and write about the strategy. Try prompts like these:

■ How will you get started on the problem?

■ What can you do if you are not sure how to begin?

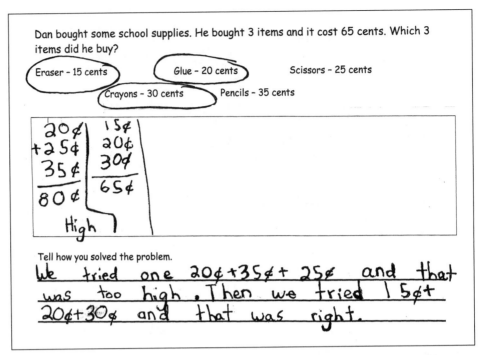

Dan bought some school supplies. He bought 3 items and it cost 65 cents. Which 3 items did he buy?

Eraser – 15 cents   Glue – 20 cents   Scissors – 25 cents

Crayons – 30 cents   Pencils – 35 cents

$$
\begin{array}{c|c}
\begin{array}{r} 20¢ \\ +25¢ \\ 35¢ \\ \hline 80¢ \end{array} &
\begin{array}{r} 15¢ \\ 20¢ \\ 30¢ \\ \hline 65¢ \end{array}
\end{array}
$$

High

Tell how you solved the problem.

We tried one 20¢ +35¢ + 25¢ and that was too high. Then we tried 15¢+ 20¢+30¢ and that was right.

Figure 9–3 *Once this student's first guess was recorded, the student was able to use revision to arrive at the correct answer.*

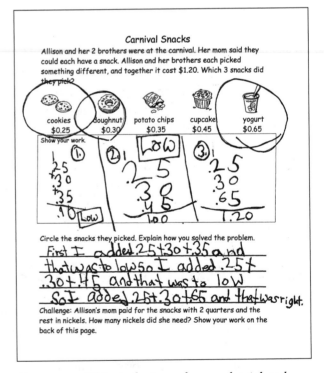

Carnival Snacks

Allison and her 2 brothers were at the carnival. Her mom said they could each have a snack. Allison and her brothers each picked something different, and together it cost $1.20. Which 3 snacks did they pick?

cookies $0.25   doughnut $0.30   potato chips $0.35   cupcake $0.45   yogurt $0.65

Show your work.

① $\begin{array}{r} .25 \\ +.30 \\ +.35 \\ \hline .90 \end{array}$ Low   ② Low $\begin{array}{r} .25 \\ .30 \\ .45 \\ \hline 1.00 \end{array}$ ③ $\begin{array}{r} .25 \\ .30 \\ .65 \\ \hline 1.20 \end{array}$

Circle the snacks they picked. Explain how you solved the problem.

First I added .25+.30+.35 and that was to low so I added .25+ .30+.45 and that was to low So I added .25+.30+.65 and that was right.

Challenge: Allison's mom paid for the snacks with 2 quarters and the rest in nickels. How many nickels did she need? Show your work on the back of this page.

Figure 9–4 *This student numbers each trial and then analyzes her guesses, noting that the first two sums were "low."*

■ How did you come up with your first guess?

■ Why is it important to revise your answers?

■ How did Guess, Check, and Revise help you solve this problem?

■ Why did you choose this strategy to help you solve this problem?

■ Why is it important to keep trying when solving problems?

Questions for Discussion

1. How does students' number sense affect their ability to effectively use the Guess, Check, and Revise strategy?

2. Can partner activities enhance the development of the thinking processes needed to effectively use problem-solving strategies? How?

3. How might teachers emphasize the importance of reasonable guesses and reasonable revisions when working on Guess, Check, and Revise thinking?

10

Strategy

Use Logical Reasoning

Reasoning is fundamental to the knowing and doing of mathematics.

—National Council of Teachers of Mathematics,
Curriculum and Evaluation Standards for School Mathematics

Logical reasoning is an important skill for solving problems. Many of the other strategies we have discussed depend on logical reasoning. Students may use logical reasoning as they create pictures or diagrams to represent confusing problem situations or as they employ guess-and-check thinking to determine solutions to problems. In many cases, it is difficult to separate logical reasoning from other strategies. Some problems, however, utilize logical reasoning as the primary problem-solving strategy. Whether it is the primary strategy, or is combined with other problem-solving strategies, logical thinking is of critical importance to students' problem-solving success.

Logic problems often seem confusing. There can be an overload of data. Students are challenged to make sense of the data and draw conclusions. Sometimes the data are straightforward (e.g., my number is an even number) and at other times the same data might be worded in a less direct way (e.g., my number is not an odd number). The data do not always directly state ideas, but can require inferencing (i.e., John does not use a bat to play his favorite sport, so John's favorite sport is not baseball since you use a bat in baseball). In this strategy, students need to practice analyzing clues or bits of information presented in the problem and then use that information to help solve the problem. Exposure to techniques like using the process of elimination can help students learn to narrow down the possible solutions so they can arrive at a logical answer. Graphic organizers such as matrices and Venn diagrams also help students organize data so they are able to clearly see the data and draw appropriate conclusions. Helping young students experience a variety of logic problems, and providing them with opportunitites to discuss ways to simplify those problems, will help them build strong logical reasoning skills.

Using Clues to Solve Logic Problems

For very young students, we can begin working on logical reasoning skills with simple problems that rely on pictures and clues.

In the problem in Figure 10–1, students use the clues and pictures to find Joey. They simply cross out the pictures that do not match the clues and one-by-one eliminate everyone except Joey. The clues are simple and straightforward. Joey has a striped shirt, a hat, and a flag.

In Figure 10–2, the clues begin to include negative statements along with positive statements. To find Mr. King, students must understand that he is wearing a tie and a hat. But the clues also say that Mr. King is not wearing glasses and does not have a moustache. Students must discern the difference between clues that describe how he looks and clues that describe how he *does not* look. Students are still supported by having pictures to cross out as they eliminate possibilities. Discussions about the wording of the clues are critical for problems in which the clues are more complex.

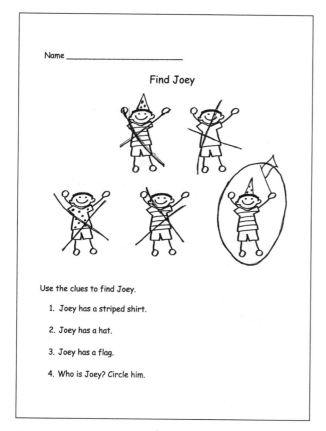

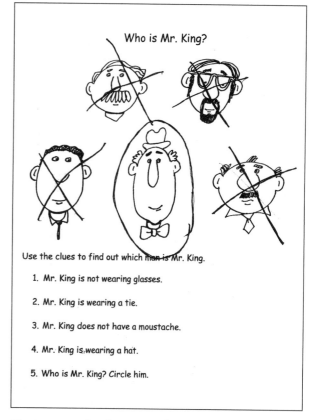

Figure 10–1 *Students follow simple clues and eliminate possibilities to find Joey.*

Figure 10–2 *Students must be careful to interpret the negative clues that describe how Mr. King does not look.*

In Figure 10–3, students now must make inferences to interpret the clues. This time, the clues do not refer to what is seen in each picture, but provide students with information that must be analyzed based on their understanding of the various foods. Which food might be hot? Which food would be eaten with your hands? Students are now challenged to make inferences as they interpret each clue and use the clues to eliminate possibilities and narrow down the choices to find the solution.

Mrs. Londo asked her kindergarten students to work with partners to find out which animal matched her clues. She gave her students pictures of five animals (horse, monkey, giraffe, camel, elephant) and asked them to listen to her clues, think about whether they could eliminate any animals based on the clues, and turn over any pictures of animals that they eliminated.

TEACHER: The animal I am thinking about cannot climb trees.
STUDENT: It can't be a monkey.
TEACHER: Why not?
STUDENT: Because a monkey is good at climbing trees, and your animal can't do that.
TEACHER: My animal cannot reach tall leaves in the trees. (*The students talked with partners to decide if any animals could be eliminated.*)

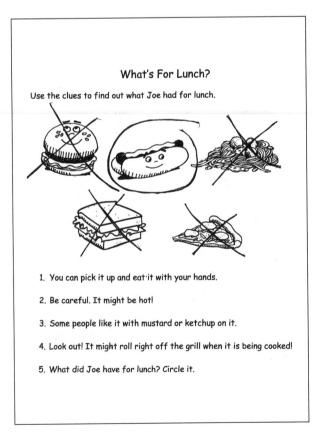

Figure 10-3 *Students must use their inferencing skills to interpret these clues.*

STUDENT: We turned over the giraffe because it has a long neck.
TEACHER: How would a long neck help?
STUDENT: It could stretch it to reach the leaves.
TEACHER: My animal does not have a hump.
STUDENT: It's not a camel. They have humps!
TEACHER: There is only one animal left, isn't there? Let's see if it fits my last clue. My animal can live on a farm and is fun to ride.

The students smiled as they held up the picture of a horse. By looking at the pictures, listening to the clues, making inferences about what each clue meant, and turning over pictures to eliminate possibilities, the students were able to process the clues, record their decisions (by turning over pictures), and find the correct solution. Working with partners gave them opportunities to talk about their thinking, and it also gave Mrs. Londo an opportunity to hear their thinking. And class discussions gave Mrs. Londo a chance to check their thinking as she required them to justify their answers.

CLASSROOM-TESTED TIP

Hands-On Logic

Hands-on activities make logical reasoning visible. Provide students with four shapes: a circle, a triangle, a rectangle, and a square (see Shape Template on the CD). Present the following clues and ask the students to put the shapes in order from top to bottom on their desks based on the clues.

Put the 3-sided shape at the top of your desk.
The circle is just below the triangle.
The shape with 4 equal sides goes at the bottom.
The rectangle is below the circle, but above the square.

Ask the students to share the order of their shapes with a partner. Ask them to discuss any differences and decide which order fits the clues. Walk around the room to visually monitor their progress. Have one pair of students explain why they placed the shapes in the order they did. Point out to students that some information is stated while other information must be inferred, or figured out. What is the 3-sided shape? Remind students that using logical reasoning involves thinking about information and making some judgments based on what is known. Use different clues to order the shapes in a different way. You might ask students to line up the shapes in a row using clues to reinforce the concepts of left, right, and between. Try similar activities, ordering different colors or familiar objects such as a pencil, crayon, eraser, and paper clip.

The Role of Inferences

Often a problem does not come right out and state the necessary data, but rather challenges students to figure out the data by "reading between the lines." Consider the following problems that require students to make inferences:

> **Darrell fed the horses 6 apples, 3 pears, and 4 carrots. How many pieces of fruit did he feed to the horses?**
> **Tia saw 2 chickens and 3 cows on the farm. How many legs did she see?**

The problems are complicated by the fact that some of the data are not directly stated. Information must be gathered based on students' understanding of the situation and their ability to draw conclusions. If we want to know how many pieces of fruit Darrell fed the horses, we must first know whether apples, pears, and carrots are fruit. If we want to determine how many legs Tia saw, we must recognize that chickens have 2 legs and cows have 4 legs. Providing opportunities for students to talk about what is stated and what is inferred will help those who are confused by the problems. Class discussions, think-alouds in which teachers model making inferences, and partner activities in which students can work together to discuss solutions are helpful instructional techniques. The ability to make inferences is a critical foundation skill for effective logical reasoning.

C L A S S R O O M - T E S T E D   T I P

Quick Inference Clues

Try some quick and easy inferencing activities to hone students' skills at using clues to infer information. You might display pictures of some fruit (e.g., banana, blueberries, apple, lemon) and provide a clue for each fruit that challenges students to make inferences to find the fruit that you have in mind. Constantly ask students to talk about and justify their thinking.

> **I put a handful of these in my cereal.** (blueberries)
> *Why couldn't it be the other fruits? What led you to choose blueberries?*

> **My fruit doesn't roll.** (banana)
> *Which fruits can roll? What do you know about the shapes of fruits that will help you?*

> **I put the core in the trash can when I was done eating my fruit.** (apple)
> *How do you know that your answer is correct? What fruits have cores that you do not eat?*

> **My fruit is sour and makes my mouth pucker when I taste it.** (lemon)
> *Which fruits are sour? Would you take a bite out of a lemon? Why not?*

Using a List to Organize Clues

When working on logic problems, it is important to record each decision that is made, so we don't forget it. In the previous problems, students' decisions were recorded by crossing off pictures or turning over cards. As problems become more abstract, our students may need to create lists on which they cross off items that are eliminated as possible answers. Consider the following number logic problem:

> **Devin gathered eggs during the egg hunt. Use the clues to figure out how many eggs she had.**
>   **It is less than 10.**
>   **It is more than 7.**
>   **It is not an odd number.**

Students can keep track of their progress toward a solution by making a list of numbers and then crossing off the rejected numbers as they analyze each clue.

It is less than 10. (*These are all possibilities. Ten is not a possibility because 10 is not less than 10.*)

    1   2   3   4   5   6   7   8   9

It is more than 7. (*That means it could not be 1, 2, 3, 4, 5, 6 or 7, so I can cross those off.*)

    X̶   X̶   X̶   X̶   X̶   X̶   X̶   8   9

It is not an odd number. (*The only numbers left are 8 and 9, and if it is not an odd number, it must be 8.*)

    X̶   X̶   X̶   X̶   X̶   X̶   X̶   ⑧   X̶

While some students may be able to do multiple steps in their heads without recording the data, many benefit from recording and eliminating data as they read, or listen to, and analyze the clues. And again, the process of recording the data ("getting it out of their heads and onto the paper") can simplify an otherwise challenging problem. Hundred charts (see Hundred Charts on the CD) and number lines (see Number Lines on the CD) are tools that allow students to "see" numbers when working with logic number problems. Students might use the number lines or hundred charts to record their ideas by crossing off or circling numbers to match the clues. Number logic problems provide practice with reasoning skills, as well as reinforcing number concepts and math vocabulary (e.g., less than, more than, odd, even).

Using a Logic Matrix

A matrix is a grid on which students record data. It is a tool for helping students organize information and keep track of their ideas as they work through the process of piecing clues together. Consider the following problem:

> **Kathy, Lisa, and Dan each have a snack. One has a banana, one has a chocolate bar, and one has raisins.**
>> **Dan does not like candy.**
>> **Kathy peels her snack.**
>> **Lisa's snack melts on a hot day.**
>> **Which snack does each child have?**

The clues are confusing. In order to find a solution, students have to first find a way to clarify the data so they can look at it clearly to draw their conclusions. Creating a grid or matrix like the one in Figure 10–4 allows them to organize the information. Students can begin the matrix by writing in the three names (Kathy, Lisa, and Dan) and the three possible snacks (banana, chocolate bar, and raisins). Then the clues are read, evaluated, and the conclusions recorded. The matrix supports students as they move toward a solution by allowing them to consider one clue at a time and to remember their conclusions since they have been recorded on the matrix.

Dan does not like candy. (*Then he must not be having a chocolate bar—I can put an x by* chocolate *on the grid.*) Notice the inference!
Kathy peels her snack. (*She must be having a banana. I can put a yes or checkmark by* banana. *That also means I can put an x by* chocolate *and* raisins *for Kathy, since she only had one snack. And I can put an x by* banana *for Lisa and Dan, since they must have had the other snacks.*) Eliminating wrong answers will help students narrow down the possibilities.
Lisa's snack melts on a hot day. (*It must be chocolate! I can put an x by* raisins *for Lisa since I now know she had chocolate.*)
   So, Dan must be having raisins for his snack!

	Banana	Chocolate bar	Raisins
Kathy	yes	x	x
Lisa	x	yes	x
Dan	x	x	yes

Figure 10–4 *Information is organized on a matrix.*

Each clue brings students closer to a solution. Inferencing helps students make sense of each clue, and the matrix helps them keep track of the clues.

Assisting primary students in understanding the use of simple grids will prepare them for effectively using the matrix for more complex problems in the intermediate grades. Modeling the use of a matrix is a good way to introduce primary students to this way of recording data. Students must understand how to read the rows and columns on a matrix. Modeling how to move through the clues, one at a time, and then record answers by placing "yes" or a happy face in the selected boxes and x's in the eliminated boxes will help students begin to see how to use the tool to record data. There can only be one *yes* or *happy face* (the chosen answer) in each row and column. That is an important understanding, as a matrix is used when students are looking for a one-to-one match (i.e., which child ate which snack), so there will be only one child matched with each snack.

Using a Venn Diagram to Organize Ideas

The ability to see logic problems through pictures and diagrams simplifies the problems. We have seen the use of pictures to help students select and eliminate items based on clues (i.e., Finding Joey from the pictures of 5 boys). We have seen the benefits of using lists and matrices to diagram problem data so that it can be seen and analyzed more easily. Another tool to make logical reasoning concrete is the Venn diagram. Consider this problem:

> **There were 7 children at Susie's birthday party. The children could have a chocolate cupcake, a yellow cupcake, or both. Five children had a chocolate cupcake. Four children had a yellow cupcake. How many children had both kinds of cupcakes?**

This problem appears very confusing. 5 + 4 = 9, but there were only 7 party guests. How can I know who might have had both kinds of cupcakes? Rather than looking for a solution, begin by helping students visualize the problem. Viewing data on a Venn diagram can help clarify this problem. One side of the diagram can be labeled "chocolate cupcakes" and the other side can be labeled "yellow cupcakes." When introducing Venn diagrams to young students, consider creating the two circles using two different-colored markers (e.g., a blue circle and a red circle). Primary students are better able to understand the overlapping section of the Venn by seeing that the words are recorded in both the blue circle and the red circle. Each child can be given seven manipulatives (e.g., colored counters) to represent the seven party guests. As students begin to represent the data on the Venn diagram, many will first place five counters in the chocolate cupcake circle. As they try to place four counters in the yellow cupcake section of the diagram, they find that they do not have enough counters. Students can be challenged to experiment with placing their counters on the diagram until they find a placement that fits the data in the problem. Working in pairs will provide students with opportunities to talk about the location and the reason for their placement choices. As students see that they can slide some counters into the center of the Venn diagram, they are able to solve the problem (see Figure 10–5).

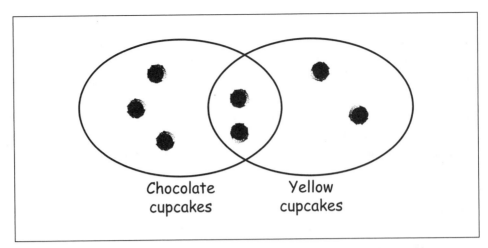

Figure 10–5 *Using a Venn diagram allows students to visualize the problem.*

CLASSROOM-TESTED TIP

Hands-on Logic with Attribute Blocks

Attribute blocks are engaging manipulatives that stimulate students' logical reasoning skills. Attribute blocks are a set of blocks that come in five shapes (rectangle, circle, square, triangle, and hexagon), three colors (red, yellow, and blue), two thicknesses (thick and thin), and two sizes (large and small). Following are two quick and easy activities that use attribute blocks to strengthen logical reasoning skills:

1. Students might work in pairs or groups to find a mystery attribute block based on a series of clues.

   My block is green. (Blocks of any other color can be removed from the set.)

   My block is not thin. (All thin blocks can now be removed. The mystery block must be thick.)

   My block is large. (All small blocks can be removed.)

   My block has 3 sides and 3 angles. (The large, thick, green, triangle is the mystery block!)

2. Attribute blocks can be used to explore similarities and differences using Venn diagrams. First, give a large Venn diagram to each group, either drawn on poster board or created by overlapping two rings or hoops. Each circle is then labeled (place an index card beside it) with one attribute (e.g., *red* by one circle, *rectangle* by the other circle). Students must sort the attribute blocks into the correct places on the Venn. All red blocks will belong in one circle, all rectangles in the other, but all red rectangles will have to be placed in the center section of the Venn. Blocks that are neither red nor rectangles will be outside the Venn.

A Look at Student Work

Model your thoughts by speaking aloud as you solve logic problems with your students. Thinking is an abstract process, but through think-alouds, students are able to hear your thinking and through the use of diagrams or graphic organizers, they can see logical thinking.

In Chapter 8 we discussed the use of pictures and diagrams to simplify problems. Combining the strategy of drawing pictures with logical reasoning helps students visualize and solve problems that appear confusing. Danny, a kindergarten student, was able to solve the following problem after drawing a picture:

> **There were 4 balloons. The green balloon was flying higher than the red balloon. The blue balloon was lower than the red balloon. The yellow balloon was higher than the green balloon. Which balloon was flying highest?**

Listening to each clue, and drawing pictures to represent the balloons, helped him make sense of the clues.

The student whose work is shown in Figure 10–6 tackled a more complicated logic problem using a matrix or grid. She used happy faces on the grid to show her answers and x's to indicate what she had eliminated. Her explanation indicates that the grid made it easier for her to remember the clues.

Figure 10–6 *This student read the clues and recorded her ideas on the matrix, allowing her to more easily solve the logic problem.*

Communicating About the Strategy

Don't forget to have students write about and talk about how they solve logic problems. Try prompts like these:

- Explain why you crossed out those items.

- Explain why you made a list on your paper.

- What does the Venn diagram show?

- Explain how the matrix or Venn diagram helped you solve the problem.

- How did recording and eliminating possibilities help you solve the problem?

- What was difficult about this problem? How did you make it easier?

Questions for Discussion

1. What is the importance of recording information when working on logical reasoning tasks?

2. How can teachers help primary students develop basic logic skills?

3. How does the use of lists, matrices, and Venn diagrams simplify logical reasoning tasks? How might primary students begin to become acquainted with the tools?

Strategy
Work Backward

Strategies are learned over time, are applied in particular contexts, and become more refined, elaborate, and flexible as they are used in increasingly complex problem situations.

—National Council of Teachers of Mathematics,
Principles and Standards for School Mathematics

Working Backward is reversing our thinking. We might work backward to solve a problem when we know how a situation ends but we don't know how it started. The strategy works well for problems such as the following:

> If I spent $2.00 to buy a toy and have $1.00 left in my pocket, how much money did I have before I bought the toy?
> If I ate half of the cookies on a plate, and there are 10 cookies left on the plate, how many were on the plate before I started eating?

In each case, we are unsure how much money or how many cookies we had to start, but can use the data in the problem to work backward to find the answer.

Understanding the Concept of Working Backward

In primary grades, working backward can simply be thought of as "undoing what was done" to get to an answer. Our goal is to help students understand how to reverse their steps to find a solution. By the intermediate and middle grades, working backward takes the more abstract form of inverse operations. Simple one-step problems are a good way to introduce this strategy to students. Students learn to reverse their math thinking—to begin with what they know about how the situation ended in order to figure out what happened at the start.

Working-backward problems can frustrate students because of unknown data at the beginning of the problem. Consider the following problem:

> **Rita went to the county fair. She used half of her tickets to ride the carousel. Then, she used 3 tickets to ride the bumper cars. She didn't have any more tickets. How many tickets did she have at the start?**

Knowing that Rita spent half of her tickets to ride the carousel is not particularly helpful if we do not know how many tickets she had prior to using half. Half is an arbitrary amount, with half of 10 being different from half of 20 or half of 4. To effectively find this solution, students will need to begin at the end of the problem, where the information is exact (0 tickets) and then reverse the actions to find out how the situation began:

> *"At the end Rita didn't have any tickets. The last thing she did was ride the bumper cars, and she used 3 tickets. Let's say that she never rode the bumper cars; how many tickets would she have? Three. Let's give her the 3 tickets back. Just before that she spent half of her tickets to ride the carousel and she was left with 3 tickets, so she must have spent 3 tickets on the carousel because that would be the other half. And if she had 3 and she used 3 we can just do 3 + 3 = 6. She must have had 6 tickets at the start!"*

A critical step in ensuring student success with this strategy is helping them check their answers. Because students often become confused when reversing their actions, a simple check will allow them to find their mistakes.

> *"Let's see if that works. If Rita had 6 tickets and she used half of them to ride the carousel, she would have 3 left. Then, she used 3 to ride the bumper cars and was out of tickets. I was right!"*

During the work-backward process, students must be able to perform math processes in inverse order, as well as apply math understandings (e.g., operations, understanding of *half*). This strategy is quite complex. Problems that require students to work backward are more likely to be found at the intermediate grades, but exposing students to simple problems at the primary level will help them begin to develop their skills.

Simplifying the Task

While second-grade students may be ready to reverse their actions to solve simple work-backward problems, younger students may not have the cognitive skills to clearly understand the process. Beginning with simple tasks to help students see that math can be done forward or backward will help prepare them for the more sophisticated work-backward tasks that will be posed in later grades.

Josh ate 12 blackberries. He had 15 blackberries left in his bowl. How many blackberries did he have when he started breakfast?

Certainly we could just add the 12 that Josh ate to the 15 that are still in the bowl (12 + 15) and get the total number, but showing students ways to reverse their thinking will help prepare them for times when working backwards may be necessary.

"So Josh had 15 blackberries left in the bowl. But he ate 12, didn't he? Could we pretend he hadn't eaten 12 and just pretend we were giving them back to him? Could we just add them to what he had left in the bowl (15 + 12)? Let's try it . . ."

Later, students might see this more complex variation:

Josh ate half of the blackberries in his bowl. He had 6 left in the bowl. How many did he have to start?

This time, we can't simply add the two numbers, because we don't know what half might be. But we can work backward and find out the missing value!

"Josh had 6 blackberries left in his bowl. He ate half. What if he hadn't eaten half? Let's give them back to him. But how many is half?"

Students benefit from visual and hands-on experiences to discover what *half* might be. Try using the overhead projector, placing 6 counters on the screen or giving students counters to explore the concept of *half*. Tell students that these 6 are *half*. Ask them what the other half would look like. Maybe try 4 counters and show 2 and 2 as *half*, and 6 counters and show 3 and 3 as *half*. Help students discover that one half will always be the same as the other half:

"He must have eaten 6 blackberries because that is half and both halves are the same!"

Try some simple problems to help primary students practice working backward. The following problems use simple numbers and require only one step, but do include words like *more*, *same*, and *twice* as many. While simpler than the *half* problem above, they challenge students to use their number sense and require them to work backward, since the initial data are unknown, until they have figured out what *3 more*, *the same number*, and *twice as many* might be.

Diane had a bag of gumballs.
She had 3 more yellow than red.
She had 6 red gumballs.
How many yellow gumballs did Diane have?

Janet had a plate of cookies.
She had the same number of chocolate as sugar.
She had 4 sugar cookies.
How many chocolate cookies were on Janet's plate?

Eddie had a sheet of stickers.
He had twice as many blue as green stickers.
He had 5 green stickers.
How many blue stickers did Eddie have?

Be sure to provide opportunities for students to talk about their thinking and provide students with access to manipulatives so they can act out their thinking and check their solutions.

CLASSROOM-TESTED TIP

Modeling Working Backward

Give each student a small bag of candy (or plastic chips to represent candy) and a copy of the bag pattern shown in Candy Bag Template on the CD. Tell the students that you are going to read them a story problem. In this problem, they will know what happens at the end of the story, but they won't know how it started. Their job is to figure out how the story began. Just like a detective, they will be using clues to re-create what happened in the story. Pose the following problem to students:

Lisa had a bag of candy. She gave 3 pieces to her sister. Then, she gave 2 pieces to her mother. She had 4 pieces of candy left. How much candy did she have to start?

Ask the students to tell you how many pieces Lisa had in her bag at the end of the problem, after giving candy to her sister and mother (4). Have each student put 4 pieces of candy (or chips) in the candy bag (or ask them to place 4 chips on the bag cutout) to represent what she had at the end of the problem. Ask the students what happened just before Lisa was left with 4 pieces of candy. (She gave 2 pieces to her mother.) Ask them to imagine that she had not done that. Tell them that together you will be "undoing what she did." Each student should put 2 more pieces of candy into the bag, as if Lisa had not given them to her mother. Ask students how many pieces of candy are in the bag now (6). Then, ask the students what Lisa did right before she gave candy to her mother. (She gave 3 pieces to her sister.) Have them put 3 more pieces into the bag as if she had never given those pieces away. Ask the students how many pieces are in the bag now (9). Ask students if Lisa gave candy to anyone else (no). Have students count how many pieces of candy were in Lisa's bag to start (9).

Ask students to check their answer by acting out the problem with the 9 pieces of candy. As you read the story to the students, have them remove the candy from the bag as it is given away by Lisa. Do the students end with 4 pieces of candy just like Lisa? If so, their answer must be correct.

Try the activity several times, changing the quantities of candy given away. Exploring working backward in a hands-on way will help students visualize the work-backward process. Emphasize the idea of starting at the end of the problem and "undoing what was done" or reversing the actions (e.g., taking back candy when Lisa gave away candy). A goal is to help students see ways to reverse their actions in mathematics, building the foundation for understanding the use of inverse operations (e.g., if she subtracted candy, then we can add candy to find out how many pieces she had at the start).

A Look at Student Work

When beginning this strategy with students, give them one-step problems to help them get a feel for the work-backward process. In the sample in Figure 11–1, the student first used coins to re-create the problem and then moved to the more abstract thinking shown in the sample. The student's writing demonstrates his understanding of reversing the process.

As students become more confident with working backward, challenge them with problems that test their thinking with words like *same as* or *twice as many*. In Figure 11–2, a student solves a problem that begins with the clue "She has 3 more yellow than red." Not knowing how many were red, the clue did not help the student solve the problem. After looking at the next clue ("She had 6 red gumballs."), the student was able to work backward to determine the answer.

In Figure 11–3, the problem begins by stating that Timmy ate half of the strawberries in a bowl. The student shows her work (a picture and addition equation) and also explains how she knew how many strawberries Timmy ate. Analyzing students' writing allows you to see if they have truly mastered the working-backward process. Asking students to both show their work and explain their thinking will help you better evaluate their understanding of the strategy.

Communicating About the Strategy

Remember to have students write and talk about the work-backward strategy as they use it to solve problems. Try prompts like these:

- How did working backward help you solve this problem?

- Why is working backward a good strategy for solving this problem?

- How can you figure out what *half* (or *same as* or *3 more*) might be?

- Why is it important to check your work after solving a problem by working backward?

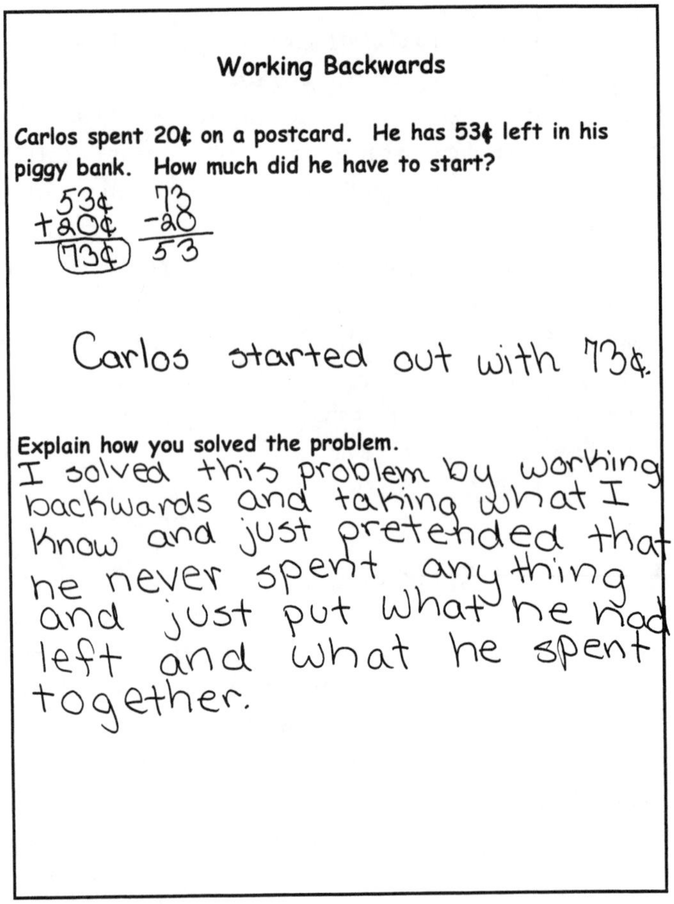

Working Backwards

Carlos spent 20¢ on a postcard. He has 53¢ left in his piggy bank. How much did he have to start?

$$\begin{array}{r} 53¢ \\ +20¢ \\ \hline \boxed{73¢} \end{array} \qquad \begin{array}{r} 73 \\ -20 \\ \hline 53 \end{array}$$

Carlos started out with 73¢.

Explain how you solved the problem.

I solved this problem by working backwards and taking what I know and just pretended that he never spent anything and just put what he had left and what he spent together.

Figure 11–1 *This student begins with the 53 cents that Carlos has left and adds the 20 cents that he spent to find the amount that he had at the start.*

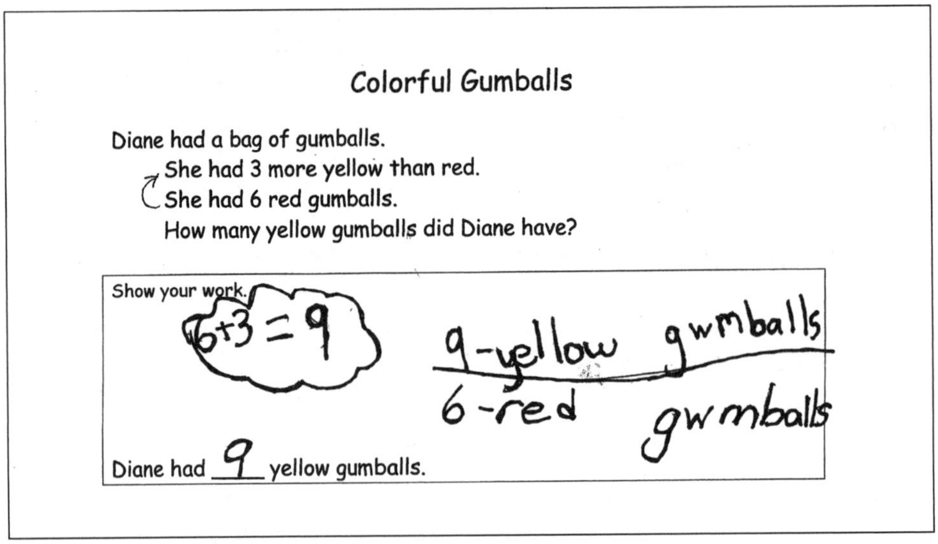

Colorful Gumballs

Diane had a bag of gumballs.
 She had 3 more yellow than red.
She had 6 red gumballs.
How many yellow gumballs did Diane have?

Show your work.

6+3 = 9

9 - yellow gwmballs
6 - red gwmballs

Diane had __9__ yellow gumballs.

Figure 11–2 *This student is able to solve the problem by considering the last clue and working backward.*

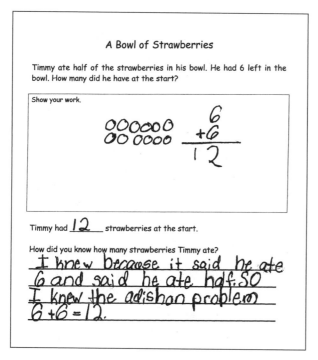

A Bowl of Strawberries

Timmy ate half of the strawberries in his bowl. He had 6 left in the bowl. How many did he have at the start?

Show your work.

OOOOOO
OO OOOO

6
+6

12

Timmy had __12__ strawberries at the start.

How did you know how many strawberries Timmy ate?

I knew because it said he ate
6 and said he ate half. So
I knew the adishan problem
6 + 6 = 12.

Figure 11-3 *This student's writing, aided by the diagram, explains how she determined the value of* half *in this problem.*

CLASSROOM-TESTED TIP

Differentiating Instruction

Students within the same classroom often have varied experience and expertise with problem-solving strategies. It is important to present lessons that allow students to explore the strategy at different levels of complexity dependent on their needs. While all students might be involved in whole-class discussions about the working-backward strategy, students can be grouped to allow some groups to explore more advanced tasks than others. Consider modifying problems for various groups to provide students with thought-provoking, but positive, experiences as they explore the strategy and refine their skills.

Beginning level—Steve bought a booklet of tickets for the carnival rides. He gave 5 tickets to Brad. He had 3 tickets left for himself. How many tickets were in the booklet that Steve bought?

Developing level—Steve bought a booklet of tickets for the carnival rides. He gave 5 tickets to Brad. Then he gave 7 tickets to Andrew. After that he had 6 tickets for himself. How many tickets were in the booklet that Steve bought?

Advanced level—Steve bought a booklet of tickets for the carnival rides. He gave half of the tickets to Brad. Then he gave 2 tickets to Andrew. He had 4 tickets left for himself. How many tickets were in the booklet that Steve bought?

Posing problems at different levels will allow you to meet the needs of all learners within your classroom. The practice problems on the CD represent varying levels of complexity. Selecting problems, or modifying problems, to match the needs of your students will help them build their problem-solving skills. Other ideas for differentiating instruction for different levels of students include the following:

- Have an additional component to the problem for groups that complete the first step (e.g., Tickets cost 10 cents each. How much did Steve pay for the booklet of tickets?).

- Vary the data in the second part of the problem to simplify or increase the complexity of the problem (i.e., Tickets cost $0.10 each—a simple computation, $0.35 each—a more difficult computation).

- Allow students access to hands-on materials (e.g., tickets) to "act out" the problem.

- Provide calculators to support students with the computations.

- While some groups work effectively on their own, others may need your input and guidance, or even some modeling, to better understand the process. Feel free to join a group and work with them to solve the problem.

Note: Cooperative group work is a great way to help all students refine their problem-solving skills. Both homogeneous and heterogeneous groups are valuable instructional formats. Heterogeneous groups (students of varied ability levels) provide an opportunity for students of different levels to learn from each other and hear each other's insights. But homogeneous groups allow you to select problems of different difficulty levels and allow faster-moving groups to extend their skills while slower-moving groups explore activities that challenge, but do not frustrate, them. Provide students with opportunities to work in both homogeneous and heterogeneous groups as they refine their problem-solving skills.

Questions for Discussion

1. Why do visual demonstrations or hand-on tasks help students better understand and remember strategies like working backward?

2. How might a teacher help students determine when working backward is a reasonable strategy to use to solve a problem?

3. How can primary teachers develop foundation skills that will support students as they move to the intermediate grades?

4. In what ways can teachers continue to challenge students as they develop their work-backward skills? How might problems be made more complex?

CHAPTER 12

Assessing Problem Solving

Assessment should not merely be done to students; rather it should also be done for students, to guide and enhance their learning.

—National Council of Teachers of Mathematics,
Principles and Standards for School Mathematics

The Role of Ongoing Assessment

Teachers traditionally viewed assessment as a culminating activity, providing information about whether each student had mastered specific math content. Fortunately, we have recognized that assessment must take place throughout the instructional process. Ongoing assessment allows us to gather information about our students' learning and monitor their progress. It also helps us make sound instructional decisions by identifying those skills and concepts that need to be retaught to ensure success for our students. Rather than being a final wrap-up of what was learned, assessment guides our instruction to ensure that we are on track with our instructional activities. A thorough understanding of problem-solving assessment guides us as we plan meaningful instructional activities that specifically address our assessment outcomes.

Because of the value of ongoing assessment in guiding the instructional process, it is critical that assessment and instruction be developed hand-in-hand. Consider our mathematics outcomes as our travel destination. Without a clear view of our students' destination, it will be difficult to determine the path they should travel to get there. But, with expected student outcomes in mind, instructional activities can be designed to move our students toward their destination. Frequent assessment activities will ensure that our students stay on the right path and will help redirect those students who might become lost along the way.

During instruction, students explore and practice their skills under the guidance and direction of the teacher. Informal assessment should occur during instruction as teachers observe students at work, listen to their discussions, and question to check their understanding. During formal assessment, however, students are given opportunities to solve problems without teacher support. Problem solving may happen in groups or individually, but it happens without teacher guidance. These assessments provide us with insight into how each student is progressing in his or her skill development. They provide information that will be essential for planning subsequent classroom lessons or valuable to share during individual student or parent conferences. In assessing problem solving, attention should be paid to both the process and the product. When analyzing students' problem-solving abilities, some very helpful types of assessment are teacher observations of the problem-solving process, interviews with students, and the evaluation of students' writing as they solve problems. Through analyzing both student behaviors and the products created during their problem-solving experiences, we can gather a wealth of information to assess our students' problem-solving abilities and plan for future instruction.

Finally, it is important to recognize that what we think we have taught is not always what students have learned. Despite our belief that a concept was fully explained or a process was sufficiently modeled, if students are still confused, it is our responsibility to think of new ways to address the concept. Ongoing assessment helps us determine when clarification, revision, or reteaching is appropriate, and allows us to celebrate our students' successes as they discover insights and demonstrate their understanding of math ideas.

The Value of Observations

Much information can be gained about students' understanding of the problem-solving process through classroom observations. Posing partner or group problem-solving tasks allows teachers the freedom to circulate through the classroom listening to their conversations and watching the ways in which they solve problems. By listening to group discussions, we can gather valuable information about our students' understanding of the problem, their ability to select and apply appropriate strategies for solving the problem, and their ability to judge the reasonableness of their plan and, ultimately, their solution. As students talk about their ideas with others, we gather information about each student's level of expertise. These observations can be informal and used simply to get a general sense of students' abilities, or they can be formal observations in which checklists are used to evaluate individual students or groups of students. The following criteria may be included in observation checklists:

- Students were able to verbalize the problem in their own words.

- Students were able to identify the important information in the problem.

- Students were able to decide on a reasonable plan for solving the problem.

■ Students checked the reasonableness of their answer.

■ Students were able to explain how they solved the problem.

Whether observations are formal or informal, they provide insight into students' understanding of the problem-solving process.

The Value of Interviews

Student interviews provide tremendous insight into students' problem-solving skills. By talking with individual students about a specific problem-solving task, the teacher gains an understanding of the student's thinking as he or she approached the task. Interviews might be formal, in which you ask a student or pair of students to meet with you to discuss a problem-solving task, or they can be informal, in which you simply join a pair, or an individual student, as they are working on a problem-solving task and ask probing questions to better understand their thinking.

While it is most effective to have some questions planned prior to conducting student interviews, a tremendous benefit to using interviews as an assessment tool is their flexibility. They allow us to modify our questions based on what we see in students' work or to probe further into their thinking based on their comments. In preparing for interviews about problem solving, consider posing questions that focus on the steps of the problem-solving process, such as the following:

What is the question you were asked to solve?
What did you already know? What did you need to find out?
Have you solved other problems like this one? Does this problem remind you of any others you have solved?
How did you solve this problem? Why?
Could you have solved the problem in another way? Explain how.
What is your answer? Does it make sense?
Was the problem easy? Hard? Why? If it was hard, what did you do to make it easier?

Some teachers prefer to schedule formal interviews in which individual students meet with the teacher for a brief conference while others are working on a designated task (e.g., center activities, independent or group math task). With their papers in hand, students are asked to explain, justify, or describe their thinking. Interviews can also be done in combination with observations, with teachers asking questions as we observe our students' actions during problem-solving tasks. Informal interviews that occur spontaneously also provide valuable assessment information. As students are working on problem-solving activities, the teacher might simply ask a few quick questions to gain additional insight into their thinking. These brief interviews are less comprehensive and might simply provide small insights that become a part of our overall assessment of student performance.

All-Pupil Response Techniques

Try an all-pupil response technique to get a quick check of your students' understanding. An all-pupil response technique is a question posed to the class in which each individual student shows his/her answer in some physical way that is easily observed by the teacher. Pinch cards (see Chapter 4) are a form of all-pupil response, because the teacher is able to quickly see each child's response by scanning the room as they pinch the operation they chose to solve a problem. Students might be given sets of color tiles and asked to hold up the color that would be next in a pattern (see Figure 12–1), or they might be asked to signal with a thumbs-up or thumbs-down to indicate whether they agree or disagree with a solution or strategy. Students might be asked to show a numerical answer (ranging from 1 to 10) by holding up that number of fingers. In all-pupil response, a quick question can yield immediate feedback about students' understanding.

Figure 12–1 *This student shows her understanding of patterns by holding up the next color in the pattern. Through all-pupil response techniques, the teacher can quickly scan the classroom to assess student understanding.*

The Value of Open-Ended Writing Tasks

Problem solving is a thinking skill. In order to monitor how students' thinking is progressing, it is important to frequently ask students to share their thoughts both orally and in writing. Students' writing allows us to recognize difficulties or misunderstandings they might be experiencing. It offers a valuable glimpse into their thinking processes and allows us to determine if they are progressing smoothly in their understanding of the problem-solving process. If young students are unable to write their own ideas, they can dictate those ideas to the teacher, who then records them on the paper. Dictating their ideas to the teacher will help students develop their communication skills and will provide a permanent record of their thoughts.

Reviewing students' writing and representations (e.g., pictures, tables, numbers) about a specific problem provides us with valuable information about their level of understanding for that specific task as well as their understanding of the problem-solving process.

When assessing students' problem-solving skills, it is critical to focus on more than the correctness of the answer. Scoring keys should address the answer as well as an assessment of students' thinking, in particular the process they took to get to that answer. A general scoring key that can be applied to a set of activities is called a *rubric*. Rubrics provide us with an assessment tool that addresses both answer and process. In addition, the rubric, when shared with students, offers them a chance to see what is expected of them before they begin a problem-solving task. It can help guide them as they work through a problem, reminding them that the answer is only part of what is being evaluated. After their task is scored, it can help them see ways in which they met, or did not meet, the assessment criteria, and it becomes a valuable tool in helping them understand how to improve their work.

A Rubric for Problem Solving

Problem solving is a multi-step task. We look for several key outcomes when assessing students' problem-solving skills.

First, students should be able to select and use an appropriate strategy. Not all students will select the same strategy, but each selection should make sense as a means to solve the problem (see Figures 12–2 and 12–3).

Second, students should be able to find a correct solution. At times, there may be more than one correct solution. Students' solutions need to make sense with the data they have at hand. In addition, students' answers need to be the result of correct math reasoning and calculations.

Third, students should be able to communicate about their problem solving. Our students' abilities to communicate their thoughts about solving problems provide us with a clearer picture of each student's level of understanding. Their writing offers insight into the process they went through to arrive at their answer. It often provides information about which we might otherwise need to conjecture. In light of the strong emphasis of the NCTM Standards regarding the development of mathematical communication, it is recommended that writing be integrated into the problem-solving

---

Making Snowmen

On the first snowy day, Mrs. Jones' class went outside to make snowmen. Each snowman needed two pine cones for eyes. How many pine cones did they need to build 10 snowmen?

What will you do to solve it?

Make a table.

Snowmen	1	2	3	4	5	6	7	8	9	10
pinecones	2	4	6	8	10	12	14	16	18	(20)

Explain what you did and what you noticed that helped you find the answer.

I made a table. I noticed we are counting by 2's. We put 2 pinecones for each snowmen.

Figure 12-2 *This student solved the problem by constructing a table and looking at the data.*

process and become a part of the scoring rubric. For very young students, we might review students' representations (e.g., pictures and numbers) to get a better idea of their thinking. And before students are able to write on their own, we might ask them to tell us what they did to solve the problem and then record their words on their papers. Even before they have the ability to write their own ideas, we should challenge them to talk about their problem-solving experiences.

Once we have determined the learning outcomes for our students, developing a problem-solving rubric becomes easy. As students look at their completed problems, they are able to see the outcomes they have met and those that they have not yet mastered. With this information in mind, they become able to revise their work to move closer to exemplary quality work.

Figure 12–4 is a rubric for scoring problem-solving tasks. First, the rubric lists the expected student outcomes, and then it outlines the criteria needed to earn scores ranging from 0 to 4.

This rubric offers a quick and easy way to assess our students' ability to solve problems. In this rubric, the selection of an appropriate strategy, the calculation of a correct answer, and the effective written explanation of the answer are the expected student outcomes. The ultimate goal is that students are able to demonstrate all three

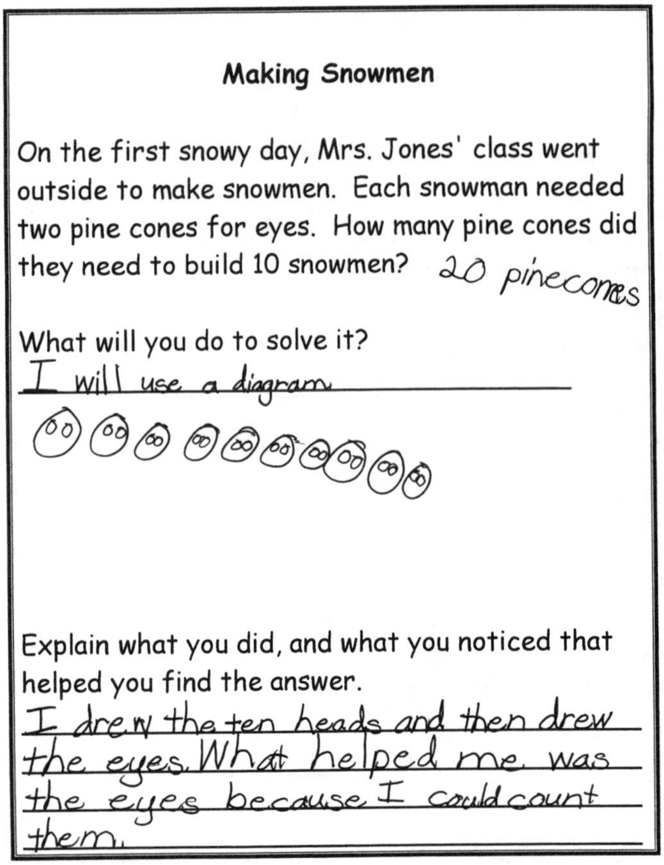

Making Snowmen

On the first snowy day, Mrs. Jones' class went outside to make snowmen. Each snowman needed two pine cones for eyes. How many pine cones did they need to build 10 snowmen? *20 pinecones*

What will you do to solve it?
I will use a diagram

Explain what you did, and what you noticed that helped you find the answer.
I drew the ten heads and then drew the eyes. What helped me was the eyes because I could count them.

Figure 12–3 *This student drew a diagram to solve the same problem. Both of the strategies in Figures 12–2 and 12–3 are appropriate and guided the students to the correct solution.*

outcomes. Students who have seen the rubric prior to the activity, or have discussed these expectations prior to the activity, will be focused on these three important outcomes. In this way, the rubric helps guide students through the problem-solving experience.

In order to score a 2 or higher, students must demonstrate their ability to select and use an appropriate strategy. Selecting a reasonable strategy is the foundation for good problem solving. If a student lacks the ability to determine *how* to solve the problem, his or her correct answer may be no more than a lucky guess. For very young students, a look at their drawings and representations will help us determine if their strategies were appropriate. Older students will be able to tell us about their strategies, shedding greater light on their thinking. Students who are able to find a correct answer based on an appropriate strategy and explain the strategy they selected will receive higher scores to correlate with their greater ability to complete the problem-solving task.

Expected Student Outcomes:

Students will be able to

1. select and use an appropriate strategy.

2. calculate a correct answer.

3. explain their strategy for solving the problem.

Problem-Solving Rubric:

4–arrived at a correct answer; used an appropriate strategy; adequately explained answer

3–used an appropriate strategy; calculated a correct answer but was unable to explain the strategy; *or* adequately explained the strategy but did not calculate a correct answer

2–used an appropriate strategy; did not find a correct answer; could not explain the strategy

1–attempted to solve the problem, but completely incorrect in attempt

0–no attempt/blank

Figure 12–4 *Rubrics are designed with expected student outcomes in mind.*

While the first two expected outcomes (selecting an appropriate strategy and calculating a correct answer) will always remain the same, the final outcome may be reworded to direct students to different types of mathematical communication. Students might be asked to tell how they found the answer, to describe a pattern that led them to the answer, or to tell why they drew a picture or made a table. In each case, the student is being asked to verbalize his or her thinking in order to assess both the math ideas and the student's ability to communicate those ideas.

For very young students, teachers might opt to simplify the rubric to focus on (1) the correct answer and (2) a reasonable approach to finding the answer. Using these two criteria, students would score two points if they arrived at the correct answer and used a reasonable approach. Students would score one point if they had a reasonable approach but did not find a correct answer (e.g., a student's incorrect answer might have been the result of a drawing or counting error, but he or she recognized that drawing a picture or counting objects was a reasonable plan for finding the answer). A student who did not have a reasonable approach for solving the problem would get no points. This simplified version allows teachers to differentiate scores for those students who are beginning to develop reasonable problem-solving approaches but may make errors in finding the answers.

Helping Students Improve Their Work

A rubric is an effective tool for guiding students in improving the quality of their problem-solving responses. Many teachers facilitate class discussions about students' methods and solutions following a problem-solving task, and then display the rubric and discuss key ideas that might have been included in their responses. Teachers might allow students to rewrite their responses following these discussions or might model the writing of an appropriate response on chart paper for all students to see.

While class discussions are an effective way to support young students in improving their work, asking them to reflect on their own written responses is also an option for more advanced students. Evaluating My Problem Solving, which is found on the CD, poses simple prompts to guide students through an analysis of their work. The prompts focus on the key components of the rubric (e.g., correct answer, reasonable approach, explanation) to help students better understand their score and reflect on ways to improve their work. Helping students develop the ability to analyze and improve their own work is our ultimate goal, as it indicates that students have internalized our expectations for their work.

C L A S S R O O M - T E S T E D   T I P

Problem-Solving Folders

Problem-solving folders contain samples of an individual student's problem-solving tasks. The teacher creates a folder for each child early in the school year and then selects several tasks each quarter to place in the folder. The folder allows teachers, parents, and students to view students' progress over the course of the school year and can even be passed along to next year's teacher at the end of the year.

Problem-solving folders that include self-evaluations are called portfolios. In portfolios, each work sample is reviewed with students and students are asked to comment on their work or set goals for future tasks. The *Evaluating My Problem Solving* worksheet on the CD is a simple technique to guide students as they reflect on their work. Both the activity and the evaluation are placed in the portfolio to document students' work and their reactions to their work. Portfolios and problem-solving folders allow teachers to view students' progress over time.

Varied Assessment

A great deal of information can be gained from frequent and varied assessment. Teacher observations, student interviews, and an analysis of students' writing can contribute important data to the assessment process. Ongoing and varied assessment throughout the teaching process will provide the information we need to make strong instructional decisions and, ultimately, create a classroom filled with successful problem solvers.

Questions for Discussion

1. Why is problem solving frequently scored using a rubric rather than simply by the correct answer?

2. What can teachers learn by asking students to talk or write about their problem solving?

3. What types of questions are appropriate during interviews to assess students' problem-solving skills?

4. What does it mean to say that we assess both product and process during problem-solving instruction?

CHAPTER 13

Problem Solving Across the Content Standards

The kinds of experiences teachers provide clearly play a major role in determining the extent and quality of students' learning.

—National Council of Teachers of Mathematics,
Principles and Standards for School Mathematics

We have been focusing on the importance of helping students develop the process skill of problem solving to allow them to effectively explore math ideas and generate solutions. We have seen that problem solving, while a critical process skill, does not stand alone. It is connected to other processes through which students learn and explore math ideas. The NCTM Process Standards (2000) of problem solving, communication, representation, reasoning and proof, and connections describe critical processes that are intertwined in our math lessons. While students are solving problems, they communicate verbally and in writing in order to process and express their ideas. They decipher representations to understand problem data or create representations to show their thinking. They use reasoning skills to make inferences, draw conclusions, and justify their solutions. They connect various math ideas in order to better understand each one, and they connect math to their lives as they explore problems in a real-world context. These five process standards interconnect in daily lessons as we develop and refine math content with our students.

While there is much overlap between the process standards, there must also be a strong connection between the process and content standards. Problem solving is a process through which students learn math content and through which they are able to apply their math skills. Providing students with experiences solving problems in various content areas is a critical way to help students practice application of these skills while actively engaging them with math content. The National Council of Teachers of

Mathematics (2000) has outlined the content standards for elementary students and has organized those standards in five content areas: number and operations, algebra, measurement, geometry, and data analysis and probability. While we help students develop their skills in the processes of problem solving, reasoning and proof, communication, representation, and connections, we are also focused on building their understanding of this content. This chapter explores the interconnectedness of the content and process standards through sample activities that illustrate a blending of content and process. Classroom activities are highlighted to illustrate problem solving in each content area. The activities are directly linked to the NCTM standards and expectations for students in prekindergarten through second grade (NCTM 2000). Resources to support you in implementing these activities are available on the accompanying CD.

Problem Solving About Number and Operations

Students in prekindergarten through second grade are beginning to explore numbers and operations. They are learning the meanings of addition and subtraction of whole numbers and are learning how to represent operations using number sentences. They are developing their computation skills and finding strategies to add and subtract whole numbers, and they are developing their skills at choosing appropriate operations to solve problems. The following activity challenges students to use their understanding of the operation of addition, their computational skills, and their problem-solving skills to explore the connections between number sentences (symbolic representations) and addition problem scenarios.

The Activity

Ms. Alexander conducted the following activity with her second-grade students during the first few weeks of school. By engaging them in discussions about the operation of addition, asking them to identify number sentences (equations) to match problem situations, and challenging them to write their own word problems to illustrate number sentences, she hoped to assess their understanding of the operation of addition, review critical addition skills, and build their understanding of addition as a problem-solving strategy.

Ms. Alexander began the lesson by posting the word *addition* (printed on a sentence strip) on the board. She asked her students to tell her something they knew about addition.

STUDENT: It's like 6 + 2 = 8.
STUDENT: It's like 5 + 5 = 10.
STUDENT: It's when you add things together.

Ms. Alexander posted a sentence strip with the words *number sentence*. "Can you tell me what that is?" she asked.

STUDENT: When you say 10 + 10 = 20.

STUDENT: It has numbers and an equal sign.

Ms. Alexander asked the students to give her some examples of addition number sentences, and she wrote one example on the sentence strip next to the words *number sentence*.

Ms. Alexander posted a sentence strip with the word *altogether*, asking students why that word would be with the addition words.

STUDENT: Adding is altogether. Like you say, "How many altogether?" when you add.

STUDENT: It's like things are all together after you add them.

Next, Ms Alexander posted the word *sum* on the board, again asking students to share their ideas about the word.

STUDENT: If you say 4 + 4 = 8, it's the 8.

STUDENT: When you add, it's like the answer.

Ms. Alexander added 4 + 4 = 8 to the sentence strip showing the word *sum* and then circled the 8 in red. Then, Ms. Alexander posted a sentence strip with the word *plus*.

STUDENT: It's when you add.

STUDENT: It's 7 plus 2.

"Do I have to write the word *plus* when I add?" Ms. Alexander asked. "Or is there a symbol I can use?"

STUDENT: You can just put the sign.

"What do you mean?" she asked. "Can you show me with your hands?" The students crossed their fingers to show the symbol for the operation of addition, and Ms. Alexander wrote it on the sentence strip next to the word *plus*.

Finally, Ms. Alexander posted and discussed the word *addends* with students, generating ideas, recording an addition number sentence, and circling the addends with a colored marker. She praised the students for their understanding of the addition vocabulary and then told students that they would be using what they knew about addition to solve math problems.

Ms. Alexander asked students to work with their partners and posed the following problem:

Allison had 10 red crayons and 5 blue crayons. How many crayons did she have?

She asked students to talk with their partners to decide on a number sentence that would solve the problem, and then to record it on their papers. She walked through the room listening to their discussions and checking their number sentences, providing help when needed. She asked students to share their number sentences. While most pairs wrote 10 + 5 = 15, one pair wrote 5 + 10 = 15. This provided an opportunity for the class to talk about what each part of the number sentence represented (the pair did accurately recognize that the 5 was the number of blue crayons and the ten was the number of red crayons) and to remind students that the order of the addends would not change the sum (the commutative property). Students were given opportunities to work with their partners to write number sentences for several addition problems. Ms. Alexander frequently commented about objects (e.g., different-colored crayons) being joined or put together as they talked about the addition scenarios, focusing students on the concept of addition.

Ms. Alexander announced that they would be reversing the task. Now, she would give them a number sentence and the students would have to write a word problem to match it. She wrote 7 + 8 = ___ on the chart paper and asked students to talk with their partners to decide on the sum. After students agreed that the sum was 15, she asked them how they figured it out.

STUDENT: I just added.
STUDENT: I counted on from 7, like 8, 9, 10, 11, 12, 13, 14, 15.
STUDENT: I added 3 more to 7, so I had ten and 5 left.
TEACHER: What do you mean? How did you make 10?
STUDENT: I took 3 from the 8 because 7 + 3 = 10. Then I only had 5 more left.

Seeing that some of the students looked confused, Ms. Alexander quickly put some color tiles on the overhead projector to model this student's thinking so that others in the class would understand her very reasonable method of breaking apart the 8 in order to first make 10, and then add the remaining 5 to find the sum (15).

"Well, you added in some different ways, but you all got 15," Ms. Alexander said. She recorded the sum to complete the number sentence. She then asked students to help her write a story to go with the number sentence.

"What should we write about?" she asked. "How about frogs?"

The students giggled.

"How many frogs should there be?" she asked, as she pointed to the number sentence.

"There could be 7 frogs," Riley said.

"Where are the frogs?" Ms. Alexander asked.

"In the grass," Riley replied.

Ms. Alexander wrote, "There were 7 frogs in the grass." Then she asked, "So, what else do we need to add?"

Ben suggested, "There were 8 frogs in the water," and Ms. Alexander recorded it.

"So, what happened next?" she asked.

"The 7 frogs went in the water!" Beth blurted out, and Ms. Alexander added her ideas to the story.

"So what is our question?" Ms. Alexander asked.

"How many frogs were in the water?" Erin answered, and Ms. Alexander finished writing the story. She read it back to the class and they agreed that their story matched the number sentence $7 + 8 = 15$.

Ms. Alexander then gave each pair of students a piece of folded construction paper. Inside their simple folded book was one of six predetermined number sentences. Their job was to work with their partners to create a story to match their number sentence and then write their story on the cover of their book. The number sentences were all addition sentences, but some involved two-digit addends while others were one-digit addends. Ms. Alexander carefully selected some simpler number sentences for a few pairs that needed more support. She circulated through the room as the students talked about their stories. She helped several pairs focus on a topic (i.e., "What are you writing about? Bees? That's a great idea! So, what can you say about the bees? What do bees do?"). She helped others focus on the operation of addition in order to write their question (i.e., "What will the bears do? How will you make it an addition problem?") Students who finished early were encouraged to draw pictures to show their addition stories on the front cover.

When all students had completed their folded books, Ms. Alexander posted the six different addition number sentences on the board. Student pairs were asked to read their stories to the class, and the class was asked to listen to each story and decide which number sentence matched it. Students were asked to explain how they knew which number sentence matched the story, being prompted to talk about the addends and sum. For $5 + 4 = 9$, Jackie and Perry wrote "5 orange dogs are running. 4 yellow dogs are playing with balls. How many dogs were altogether?" For $14 + 3 = 17$, Kyle and Shana wrote, "We had 14 cakes. We baked 3 more. How many did we have?" Ms. Alexander continually supported and highlighted their understanding of groups *coming together* in their addition stories.

About the Math

This activity challenged students to connect their understanding of addition equations (the symbolic representations) and their understanding of the operation of addition (the problem-solving scenarios). Students were asked to verbalize their understanding of the operation of addition through discussions of key addition vocabulary. Early in the lesson, students were given addition scenarios and asked to represent the stories in symbolic form through numbers sentences. Later in the lesson, students were given the symbolic form and were challenged to construct stories to demonstrate their understanding of the operation.

Students were encouraged to work with partners throughout the lesson to provide them with many opportunities to express their understandings about addition, hear each others' ideas, and clarify the number sentences or story problems. The teacher asked many questions to stimulate students' thinking and modeled the writing of a word problem before asking students to work with partners to write their own.

While the activity strengthened students' understanding of addition, it also provided foundational skills for effective problem solving as students were challenged to explore the concept of addition through problem-solving contexts. Students were given practice in developing equations to solve story problems. In addition, the teacher gained insight into students' understanding of the concept of addition, as well as their problem-solving skills related to using addition to solve problems, by listening to their stories and comments.

Problem Solving About Algebra

An important goal for students in prekindergarten through second grade is the understanding of patterns. The recognition and extension of patterns is a fundamental algebra skill. Focusing on patterns challenges primary students to explore relationships between numbers, shapes, or colors. The ability to recognize and extend patterns is also an important problem-solving skill. Primary students should have opportunities to explore patterns related to sounds, shapes, colors, and numbers. In the following problem, kindergarten students were challenged to analyze and describe simple patterns as they developed an understanding of the concept of pattern and repetition.

The Activity

The teacher, Mrs. Montgomery, posed the following problem to her kindergarten class:

> **There were some little bears walking to the park. First a red bear, then a blue bear, then a red bear, then a blue bear . . .**

As Mrs. Montgomery posed the problem, she placed colored bears on the overhead projector to illustrate her story. She asked the students, "Which bear was next in line?"

STUDENT: A red one.
TEACHER: How do you know?
STUDENT: Because it was red, blue, red, blue, so red is next.
STUDENT: It's a pattern!
TEACHER: What do you mean? What's a pattern?
STUDENT: It's red, blue, red, blue.
STUDENT: It's over and over and over.
TEACHER: So you could tell what came next from something I said, something that repeated?

The students nodded. Mrs. Montgomery shared another story, this time lining up green and yellow bears. The students correctly predicted the next bear for her line. Mrs. Montgomery asked them to tell her the pattern. Together, they repeated the pattern "green bear, yellow bear, green bear, yellow bear . . . ".

"What repeats in this pattern?" she asked, focusing them on identifying the repeating part of her pattern.

"It's always green, then yellow," Stevie said.

Mrs. Montgomery told the students to observe carefully so they could figure out the answer to her next problem.

Jess is making a necklace. She is using circle and square beads to make her necklace. The beads create a pattern. Which bead should be next on her necklace?

She drew a line on the overhead to represent the necklace string and then placed a square, then a circle, then a square, then a circle on the string to represent the beads on the necklace. She gave each student a bag of foam circles and squares and asked them to hold up the shape that should be next in her pattern. Students grabbed a square from their bags and held it up. She repeated this several times with different patterns, having students show her the next shape for her pattern, each time asking them questions like "Why do you think that shape is next?" and "Tell me the pattern you see." She then created patterns with more complexity (e.g., ABB patterns), such as square, circle, circle, square, circle, circle . . . Most of the students selected the correct shape to complete the necklace, but Mrs. Montgomery noticed several students who were not able to complete her patterns correctly.

Mrs. Montgomery then asked if the students could solve a problem on their own. She reminded them to observe carefully and to think about patterns, and gave each student a piece of paper with a horizontal line to represent the necklace string. She read the following problem as she placed the initial shapes on the overhead to model the problem:

Alice is making a necklace. First she used a circle, then a square, then a circle, then a square. What shape should she put on the string next?

She asked the students to use the shapes to show the pattern on their papers, to add the next shape in the pattern, to check to see if their partner picked the same shape, and when they were sure of their pattern, to glue the shapes to their paper. She asked students to circle the shape that Alice would put next in her pattern (the answer to their class problem). As students began to work, Mrs. Montgomery supported the students she had identified in the previous part of the activity as having difficulty completing the patterns. She pointed to each shape and asked them to tell her the shape names. She asked them to listen as they named them and asked them if they heard anything repeat. As the other students finished gluing their patterns, Mrs. Montgomery moved through the room asking students to describe their patterns. She wrote their comments on their papers. After each child dictated their pattern to her, she asked the student to use the shapes to create a pattern of their own. She gave additional shapes (e.g., stars, ovals, hearts) to some students to challenge their thinking and to allow them to create more complex patterns (see Figure 13–1). Again, Mrs. Montgomery prompted the few students who were struggling with identifying the pattern. Again, she asked students to dictate their patterns to her so she could assess their understanding. At first glance, one pattern appeared to have errors, but by asking the student to describe his pattern, Mrs. Montgomery realized that he did not record left-to-right, but

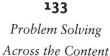

Figure 13–1 *This student solves problems by creating shape patterns.*

rather in a circular fashion going from left to right in one row and then back from right to left in a second row. After having him describe his pattern to her, she recognized his understanding of the pattern.

Several students, while understanding how to complete a pattern, became confused when asked to generate a pattern of their own. Mrs. Montgomery asked Diane to describe her pattern (square, circle, triangle) and then used questions to guide her in the development of a pattern. Diane recognized the need to modify her pattern to include repetition and revised it to square, circle, triangle, square, circle, triangle.

Mrs. Montgomery ended the activity by asking students to tell her about patterns.

STUDENT: They are like circle, square, circle, square.
STUDENT: They are the same over and over.
STUDENT: You can tell what will be next.
STUDENT: They repeat a lot.

"And they help you solve problems," Mrs. Montgomery added. "They helped us figure out how the bears walked to the park and how Jess and Alice made their necklaces."

About the Math

The major focus of this task was the recognition and understanding of color and shape patterns, and the use of patterns to solve problems. Through recognizing and extending patterns, students were able to effectively solve simple problems. The patterns were all repeating patterns, but varied from AB patterns to ABB patterns or ABC patterns.

The teacher modeled the problem situations using visual demonstrations on the overhead and providing manipulatives for the students. The visual and hands-on experiences allowed the students to see the patterns that were created. The use of an all-pupil response strategy (e.g., hold up the shape that would be next in the pattern) allowed the teacher to assess whether all students understood the concept, and allowed her to identify and provide individual support to struggling students during the remainder of the lesson.

Asking students to glue the shapes to create necklace patterns provided an initial experience with recording problem data in order to better see it and solve the problem. In addition, creating the patterns allowed the teacher to better assess each child as she asked each child to dictate the pattern to her so she could record their words on their paper. As students finished extending the class pattern, they were further challenged to create their own pattern. This allowed students to move at their own pace, with some still working on the given pattern and others creating patterns of their own. And some students were given additional shapes to provide a more challenging variation of the task.

Problem Solving About Measurement

Students in prekindergarten through second grade are learning to measure objects with non-standard and standard units. They are beginning to explore ways to measure the length of objects by using multiple units of the same size (e.g., connecting cubes). In addition, they are learning to make closer predictions, or estimates, of the unknown length of an object by comparing it to the known length of another object (a benchmark). In the following problem, students were challenged to use connecting cubes to predict and measure the length of various items.

The Activity

Miss Roosevelt began the lesson by writing the word "predict" on the board. She asked her first-grade students to talk with a partner about what it meant to predict.

STUDENT: It is like when it might snow.
TEACHER: Who predicts if it might snow?
STUDENT: The TV.
TEACHER: Do they know for sure that it will snow?
STUDENT: Sometimes it won't snow.
TEACHER: So they think it might snow when they predict? *(Many students nod in agreement.)*
TEACHER: What else can you tell me about predicting?
STUDENT: You guess.
TEACHER: How is a prediction like a guess?
STUDENT: You don't really know.

Miss Roosevelt asked the students if they had done any predictions together in class.

STUDENT: We predicted that we would spin a red.
TEACHER: When we worked with the spinners, we predicted, didn't we? We predicted what we thought would happen. Were we always right?
STUDENT: We were wrong sometimes.

Miss Roosevelt told the class that today they would be making predictions about the length of things in their classroom. She reminded them that predictions are not always correct, but that we want them to be close. She showed her students a few connecting cubes and asked them to predict how many cubes it might take to measure the length of a strip of construction paper that was taped to the board. She asked the students to talk with their partners and decide on their prediction together. Students' responses ranged from 7 cubes to 50 cubes. She recorded their predictions on chart paper.

Miss Roosevelt looked at the different predictions and told students that she thought they needed some help to get closer to the measurement. She held up a pencil and asked students how many cubes long they thought it would be. Sean said that he thought it was 7 cubes long, so Miss Roosevelt connected 7 cubes and placed the row of cubes next to the pencil. Miss Roosevelt asked the students to describe what they saw.

STUDENT: It's not long enough. The pencil is bigger.
TEACHER: So let's think about this. Seven cubes is not long enough. How long do you think the pencil is? Talk to your partners and try again.

Darnell guessed that it was 11 cubes long, so Miss Roosevelt took 11 cubes, linked them together, and placed them next to the pencil, but the row of cubes was too long this time.

"Now, what do we do?" she asked her students. Chase suggested 10 cubes, so Miss Roosevelt placed a row of 10 cubes next to the pencil and it was the same length as the pencil.

"How did you know it was 10?" she asked.

Chase replied, "It was just a little too long last time."

Miss Roosevelt asked the students what helped them come up with a closer prediction.

STUDENT: We tried too big and too small, so we knew.
STUDENT: We looked when you put the pencil next to it.
STUDENT: We kept trying and then we got it.

Miss Roosevelt praised the students for paying attention to each guess and adjusting their guesses until they figured out the correct number of cubes. "When 7 was too few, you tried more, didn't you? And when 11 was too many, you tried 10. You were observing and thinking and you got the right answer. So, what about the length of the strip of paper on the board? Will knowing how many cubes we used to measure a pencil help us figure out how long the strip of paper might be?" She asked students to look at the predictions that were recorded on the chart paper and to think about what they knew about the pencil and to decide if any of their predictions would not be close to the measurement of the paper. Ellie and Kate, who had initially predicted 10, said that it would be "more cubes because a pencil is 10 and the paper is bigger." Jamal and Victor said that 50 was "way too many because that would go all across the board."

Miss Roosevelt asked the pairs to give her a new prediction for the length of the paper. Jamal and Victor guessed it would be 20 cubes. Miss Roosevelt asked them to connect 20 cubes and to place it next to the paper strip. The cubes were longer than the paper strip.

"What do you know now?" she asked. She asked students to think about what they observed and gave each pair a set of cubes. She asked them to predict the length of the paper strip and then to connect the number of cubes that they believed would match the paper strip. She asked for one group to come forward to check their row of cubes against the paper strip.

Jay and Elaine placed their 18 cubes against the strip and found that their row of cubes was too long. Miss Roosevelt told the students to talk to their partners and adjust their rows of cubes. She walked through the room and watched students add or remove cubes from their rows, asking them questions to check their thinking. She called another pair to check their prediction, but it was too short (14 cubes) and again asked pairs to talk together and adjust their rows based on what they saw. Finally, Ali and Jen placed their row of 16 cubes next to the paper strip and it was exactly the same length. Miss Roosevelt asked them to tell her how they knew it would be 16 cubes. Jen shared, "It was bigger than 14." Ali added, "We kept making ours bigger and smaller when we saw other rows next to it."

Miss Roosevelt praised the students for listening to each other, thinking about what they observed, adjusting their answers, and for continuing to try even when they had some guesses that were not correct. Miss Roosevelt ended the lesson by asking for one more prediction: "If a pencil is 10 cubes, and the paper is 16 cubes, how many cubes long is my desk?"

"It is more than 30," Apache said, "because it is lots more than the paper."

About the Math

This task required students to measure length using non-standard units. It also required them to predict measurements. Initially many students were unable to make reasonable predictions for the length of the paper strip, but the teacher supported them by developing a benchmark (the length of a pencil). In addition, the teacher modeled the use of guess, check, and revise thinking to assist students in making reasonable adjustments to their predictions.

The teacher recorded the students' initial predictions and asked them to revisit and modify those predictions based on their observations during the lesson. The lesson was done with hands-on materials. Initially the teacher modeled with connecting cubes, but then students were able to use cubes to check and adjust their predictions.

Students were asked to work with partners so they could hear each other's ideas and talk about each prediction. In many cases, one partner helped the other decide on a reasonable prediction. The teacher frequently asked students to talk about their thinking as they modified the measurements. The teacher summarized the key ideas at the end of the activity, and specifically praised students for their problem-solving skills (guess, check, and revise thinking) and attitudes (being persistent). Through this problem exploration, students had opportunities to test and refine their understandings of measurement, as well as practice their problem-solving skills, specifically their use of guess, check, and revise thinking.

Problem Solving About Geometry

Students in prekindergarten through second grade are learning about two-dimensional geometric shapes. They are learning to name shapes, to recognize the attributes of shapes, to draw representations of shapes, and to compare shapes. They are beginning to experiment with putting shapes together to make new shapes or with taking them apart, and are beginning to recognize the use of transformations (flips, slides, and turns) when creating new shapes. Through the primary years, they are deepening their understanding of the characteristics of two-dimensional shapes. In the following task, students are challenged to solve problems that require them to construct congruent shapes, applying their skills with flips, slides, and turns.

The Activity

Ms. Short began the lesson by asking her second-grade students to tell her about several geometric shapes. She placed a triangle pattern block on the overhead and asked students to tell her the name of the shape. They quickly told her it was a triangle, and she asked, "How do you know?"

"Because it has 3 sides," Debi said.

"It has 3 points," Dan added.

Ms. Short pointed to the "points" and restated Dan's comments using slightly different vocabulary: "So it has 3 corners or angles." Ms. Short then placed a trapezoid pattern block on the overhead and asked students to name the shape. One student said "hexagon," and another said "tentathon," but none could come up with the name.

TEACHER: How many sides does it have?
STUDENT: 4.
TEACHER: What shapes have 4 sides?
STUDENT: Square.
TEACHER: Is this a square?
STUDENT: No.
TEACHER: Why?
STUDENT: The sides aren't the same.

TEACHER: So a square has sides that are equal length? Is it different from a square in any other ways?

STUDENT: It doesn't have straight-up sides.

TEACHER: So the corners don't look like the corners of a square? Are there any other shapes with 4 sides?

STUDENT: Rectangle.

TEACHER: Is this a rectangle?

STUDENT: No, it doesn't have straight-up sides.

TEACHER: So this shape has a different kind of corner or angle? We call it a right angle. Those are good observations. It is like a square and rectangle in some ways, but different in other ways. This shape is called a trapezoid.

Ms. Short wrote the word *trapezoid* next to the shape on the overhead. Then she placed a rhombus pattern block on the overhead.

"Does anyone know what this shape is called?" she asked.

Students responded that it was "a diamond," "a crystal," and "a kite without a tail." Ms. Short asked the students how many sides the shape had and they agreed that it had 4 sides, so she probed further. "So is it a square? Is it a rectangle? Is it a trapezoid?"

She asked students to talk to their partner to discuss how the rhombus was alike and different from the other shapes with 4 sides. After allowing them a few minutes to talk, she asked for them to share their ideas.

STUDENT: The sides are all the same like a square.

STUDENT: The corners aren't like the corners of a square or rectangle.

STUDENT: The corner is on top, but on a square it is on the sides.

Ms. Short turned the rhombus so that an angle was not on the top and asked if it was now a square. The students agreed that it was still not like a square. She put a square pattern block on the overhead and turned it so that the angle was at the top, and asked if it was still a square. The students agreed that it was. Ms. Short asked if there was anything else they could tell her about the shape.

STUDENT: It's like a square that is stretched out at the corners.

Ms. Short placed the square and rhombus side-by-side and told students that it was called a rhombus.

Ms. Short then placed a hexagon pattern block on the overhead. Students' hands immediately shot up and they began to try to name the shape suggesting it was an octagon, a hedagon, a pentagon, until Ms. Short labeled the shape a hexagon. Students talked about the number of sides and angles on the hexagon. Ms. Short told students that they would be using the shapes (hexagon, trapezoid, rhombus, triangle) to solve some problems. On each table (4 to 6 desks pushed together), she placed a plate filled with pattern blocks (see template on the CD) and then posed this problem:

Can you make a trapezoid without using the trapezoid block? Find 2 different ways to do it.

She asked students to work with partners to solve the problem. She clarified that they must make a shape the exact size of the trapezoid by using different pattern blocks. She asked them how they could be sure that their trapezoid is exactly the same size and shape as the trapezoid pattern block. One student said he would "measure it," another said she would "put my blocks right on top of the trapezoid block," and another said he would "trace it and fill in the space with other blocks." Students began putting shapes together to create a trapezoid.

After a few minutes, Ms. Short asked them to share the different ways they found. As students talked, she used the overhead pattern blocks to show their way of creating a trapezoid. One pair used 3 triangles. She placed them on the overhead and commented that she couldn't make a trapezoid. "No, turn the middle one," David said. She asked David to show her and he turned the triangle to create the trapezoid.

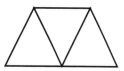

"Oh, so turning the shapes will help you find new ways?" Ms Short asked.

Allison shared another way to create a trapezoid using a rhombus and a triangle. Ms. Short put the pattern blocks on the overhead to illustrate her idea. Greta suggested another way with a rhombus and a triangle and Ms. Short took 2 different pattern blocks and showed that way right next to Allison's idea. "Are these different ways?" she asked.

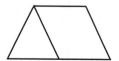

Students disagreed as to whether they were the same or different. Ms. Short put just the rhombus on the overhead and flipped it. "Is it still a rhombus?" she asked. "Is it the same size and shape?" They all agreed that it was. Then, she flipped Allison's trapezoid (the rhombus and triangle) and it looked just like Greta's trapezoid. "Are these the same?" she asked. Many students said yes, although some were still confused. "If you can turn it or flip it, we will call it the same, so Allison and Greta both found the same way to make a trapezoid. It can be tricky, so you may need to turn or flip your trapezoids, just to be sure," Ms. Short added.

Ms. Short then posed another problem for the students.

Can you make a hexagon without using the hexagon block? Find at least 3 different ways.

She asked students to work with their partners again and told them that they might even find more than 3 possible ways. She asked them how they will remember the ways they found. Several students suggested drawing the different ways, so Ms. Short asked them to trace and draw their different hexagons. She reminded them that each hexagon should be different from the others they make. As students worked, she circulated through the room asking questions or offering assistance (see Figure 13–2). For one pair, who were stuck with just one possibility, she reminded them to turn or flip the shapes to try to find different possibilities. For another pair, who quickly got 3 possibilities, she challenged them to find as many as they could. After allowing time for their investigation, she asked them to check to be sure all of their hexagons were created in different ways, and to record the number of ways they were able to create a hexagon. She then conducted a brief class discussion as students shared different possibilities and she modeled them using the overhead pattern blocks.

"What did you do so you wouldn't be confused about whether you'd already made that hexagon?" Ms. Short asked.

"We drew the ones we made," Dan said.

"We reminded each other," David said.

Ms. Short praised the students for working together to solve the problem and for remembering to record their data to help make a difficult problem easier to solve.

About the Math

This task began with the teacher asking students to discuss the characteristics of various two-dimensional shapes. Students compared unknown shapes to familiar ones, and they learned new shape names. The task also required students to create trapezoids

Figure 13–2 *The teacher asks questions to prompt students' thinking and assess their understanding.*

and hexagons from other shapes. Students were challenged to apply their understanding of transformations (flips, slides, and turns) as they created the congruent shapes. To ensure that the shapes were unique, students traced the original shape and placed the new pattern blocks within the traced outline.

To solve this problem, students used both physical models and drawings. Both helped them visualize the ideas. Sharing their ideas with partners, and as a whole class, allowed them to identify a greater number of possibilities. The teacher frequently illustrated their ideas using transparent pattern blocks on the overhead projector, so that all students could follow the class discussions.

Tracing to record each shape allowed students to keep track of what had been done (see Figure 13–3). Several pairs identified duplicate tracings and crossed one out on their papers. Their drawings were instrumental in helping them compare for the uniqueness of each solution. One pair used the drawings to help them organize their attempts. They created hexagons with 2 trapezoids, with 3 rhombi, and with 6 triangles. One student commented, "We need to make a hexagon with some of each." Recording their possibilities helped them figure out an approach for finding more possibilities.

Persistence was an essential ingredient to success in this activity. While students found it easy to create the first few possibilities, the task got increasingly difficult, and sometimes frustrating, as they had to find more unique ways to make a hexagon. The teacher encouraged them, praised their efforts, recognized the complexity of the

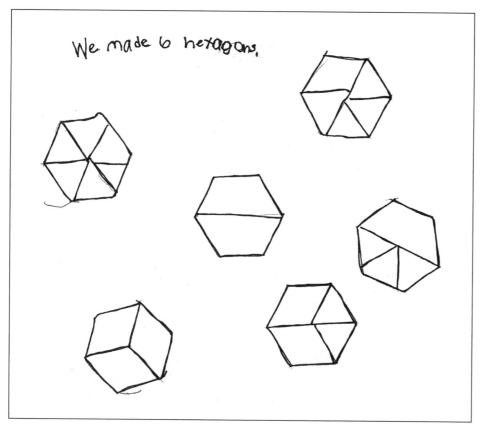

Figure 13–3 *This student traced the shapes to keep track of his solutions.*

task, and did not focus on which group had the most possibilities. The teacher's comments and questions guided and supported the students throughout the problem-solving task.

Problem Solving About Data and Probability

Primary students are developing an understanding of basic graphing concepts. Students in prekindergarten through second grade are learning to gather and display data in order to answer questions. They are learning to represent information on pictographs, to describe what they see on the graphs, and to analyze the information in order to draw conclusions about the data. In the following activity, first-grade students gathered data about themselves to create and analyze a class pictograph about their favorite summer snacks.

The Activity

Mr. Rinehart began the lesson with his just-entering-first-grade students by talking about the summer. He talked about how hot it was during the summer and how nice it was to have a cool snack after being outside in the heat. He talked about some favorite snacks that cooled him off: juicy watermelon, a cool fudge bar, and a dish of cold ice cream.

Mr. Rinehart said he wondered what his students would pick if they were able to pick their favorite summer snack. "If I were going to the store to buy some snacks for our class, I wouldn't know what to buy for you," he said.

The students began raising their hands. He asked them, "How could I find out what snack you would like if you could choose a slice of juicy watermelon, a cool fudge bar, or a dish of cold ice cream?" The students began calling out their favorite snacks.

"But I need to know what everyone will want. I would need to be sure I bought just the right amount at the store. What if 10 people wanted a fudge bar and I only bought 5 of them? How could I figure out what you each want?" he asked.

One student responded that he could ask them. Mr. Rinehart replied, "I could do that," and began pointing to various students as they said the snack they would choose.

"Wait a minute," he said. "I am getting confused. I forgot what she said. I can't remember all of this!"

"You could make a list," Emma suggested.

"That's an idea," said Mr. Rinehart. "I could write it down so I could see it better, get a better idea of what I should buy at the store. Let's see if we can record what you would choose for a snack. Let's make a pictograph!" (The students had been introduced to a pictograph several days prior to the activity.)

 Mr. Rinehart brought pictures of the different snacks to each table and asked students to pick the snack they would choose (see templates in the *Across the Content Standards activities* on the CD). After each student had selected his or her snack, he placed chart paper on the board and asked what they should call the graph. The class labeled it "Our Favorite Summer Snacks." Mr. Rinehart labeled the rows *watermelon, fudge bar,* and *ice cream* and then asked each group to tape their snack picture on the pictograph. "Now, will this help me figure out which snacks to buy?" he asked, and the students nodded.

When the graph was complete, Mr. Rinehart asked, "So how many slices of watermelon do I need?" Students began to raise their hands, but Mr. Rinehart asked the class to show him how many slices he would need by holding up that number of fingers. He scanned the room and saw most students holding 3 fingers (correct answer) and asked them how they knew that. "You count the watermelon," Jenny answered. Mr. Rinehart asked her to show him and she approached the board and counted the 3 pictures on that row of the graph.

Mr. Rinehart then asked the students to show him, with their fingers, how many fudge bars he would need to buy (5) and how many dishes of ice cream he would need to make (10), always asking students how they got their answer. Mr. Rinehart also asked students to tell him what he needed to buy the *most* of and the *least* of and had students explain how they got their answers.

Next, Mr. Rinehart asked students to look at the class pictograph to help him with any other supplies he might need to buy. He asked them if he should buy spoons and how many they would need. "Do you need spoons to eat your slice of watermelon?" he asked. "Do you need spoons to eat a fudge bar?" he added. "How about your dish of ice cream? Do you need a spoon for that?"

He asked students to whisper with the others at their table to decide how many spoons they would need and to be sure they could justify their answers by telling him how they figured it out. As students whispered in their groups, he listened to their talk. He polled each group, and all suggested that he needed 10 spoons. "But how do you know that? I don't see spoons anywhere on our graph," he said.

"But you need them for ice cream and it's 10!" said Sara.

Mr. Rinehart replied, "So you could figure out that I needed 10 spoons by looking at our graph? You knew we wouldn't need spoons to eat watermelon or fudge bars. You are good thinkers!"

Mr. Rinehart then posed another question to the groups. He explained that he would need to clean up after the party and wondered how many sticks he would have to clean up. Again, he asked students to whisper in their teams. Again he listened to their talk and asked them to justify their answers. "You only have sticks in fudge bars," Riley explained.

Finally, Mr. Rinehart posed one last question. He asked students to figure out how many napkins they would need. He mentioned that watermelon was sticky and drippy. He commented that fudge bars drip, and ice cream can be messy. Students worked in teams and whispered their ideas about the napkin problem, and then Mr. Rinehart stopped them. He gave each student a worksheet (see *Across the Content Standards* activities on CD) and reviewed the task with them. They would need to fill in the number of people who chose each snack in the space next to each snack graphic, draw the snack picked most and the snack picked least, and write the number of spoons needed, sticks that would be left, and napkins that would be needed. Mr. Rinehart told the students that they could use the bottom of the paper to write anything down that might help them solve the napkin problem.

As the students began working independently, he circulated through the room, observing their work. He frequently asked students how they figured out the napkin problem and encouraged them to write how they solved it (see Figure 13–4). Finally,

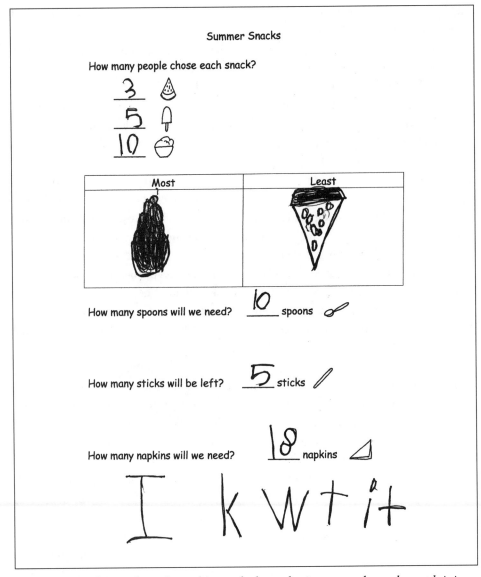

Figure 13–4 *This student shows his work through pictures and words, explaining that "I counted it."*

he asked students to share how they solved the problem with the rest of the class. Many students commented that they counted the pictures on the pictograph. Some students placed tally marks on their papers and then counted those. One student said she added to find the answer.

Mr. Rinehart praised the students for their group work, their math talk (explaining their answers) and their thinking as they answered questions (i.e., about spoons, sticks, and napkins) even when the data were not on the graph.

About the Math

In this task, students had opportunities to gather data about themselves and represent that data on a pictograph. The teacher began with a question, to set the purpose for gathering and displaying data. Being one of the class' initial exposures to creating pictographs, the teacher guided the development of the graph using lots of math talk as he titled and labeled the pictograph.

Students were actively engaged in the thinking components of the activity through all-pupil response formats (showing their answers by holding up fingers), and whispering answers and strategies in teams. The teacher asked questions throughout the lesson to guide their thinking and routinely asked students to explain their answers. The questions focused students on key graphing concepts including the ability to describe data on the graph using numbers and words like *most* and *least*. The final questions challenged students to make inferences (logical reasoning) as they determined the number of spoons, sticks, and napkins.

The teacher supported students with both whole-class and small group discussion as they solved the problems, but also transitioned to independent work near the end of the lesson in order to assess each student's understanding. The teacher asked students to record how they determined the answer to the napkin problem, but followed up with asking them to verbally explain their thinking, as many of the first-grade students had a difficult time putting their ideas in writing. The activity effectively blended data analysis skills with problem-solving skills as the students used the pictograph as a tool to gather data to solve a problem.

Linking Problem Solving and Math Content

Problem-solving activities provide students with opportunities to explore math content and expand their understanding of that content, to apply math skills to problem situations, and to practice their use of problem-solving strategies. Whether problems focus on numbers and operations, algebra, geometry, measurement, or data and probability, students benefit from opportunities to explore math content through problems. When problem-solving tasks are carefully selected, they serve to expand and refine students' understanding of the problem-solving process as well as their understanding of math content.

Questions for Discussion

1. How are problem-solving skills reinforced during these tasks?

2. What should the teacher consider when selecting problem tasks? What considerations during planning would result in more effective problem-solving lessons?

3. How does integrating content and process enhance student learning?

4. In what ways should teachers support students as they engage in problem-solving lessons?

5. How might the teacher support struggling students and challenge gifted students during problem tasks?

Accepting the Challenge

Teaching mathematics well is a complex endeavor, and there are no easy recipes.

—National Council of Teachers of Mathematics,
Principles and Standards for School Mathematics

Teaching students to become effective problem solvers is both the goal and the challenge of elementary mathematics instruction. The goal is for students to solve problems, not to perform isolated math drills. Through the process of solving problems, students recognize the meaningfulness of the math we teach, identify ways to apply math skills to find solutions to problems, and gain greater insight into the mathematics they are exploring. Problem solving engages students in the study of mathematics. It motivates them, stimulates their curiosity, and helps them gain insights.

But problem solving is challenging for our students, as it requires them to understand math skills and concepts and to develop the thinking skills necessary to apply those skills and concepts to problem situations. Problem solving is not something that can be memorized. Each problem task requires thought, discussion, planning, and an understanding of which math skills to apply and how to apply them to solve the problem.

We are beginning to recognize the importance of teaching through problem solving, of allowing students to explore math ideas through problem tasks. And we are recognizing the importance of focusing on the teaching of problem-solving skills to support students as they develop a repertoire of strategies for approaching problems. We have identified skills and strategies that guide students through the problem-solving process and assist them in organizing needed data. Discussions, group work, and writing in mathematics class have allowed students to share their thinking processes and strengthen their understanding of the skills they are acquiring.

Working Together to Build Effective Problem Solvers

Students benefit from ongoing experiences with problem solving, and schools that work together to support students' problem-solving skills are able to offer students the consistency of a problem-solving focus across grade levels. When students explore math through problem tasks and discuss their problem-solving skills from year to year, they are able to build on prior experiences and refine their understandings. It is our individual responsibility, as well as a school responsibility, to develop our students' problem-solving skills, refine our teaching skills, and provide the most appropriate math education for our students.

C L A S S R O O M - T E S T E D   T I P

School-wide Focus

Consider working together within your school to strengthen the problem-solving skills of students at all grade levels. Make problem solving a priority within your math classrooms. Try these school-wide activities:

- Develop school-wide programs to motivate students (e.g., Problem-of-the-Week announcements or school-wide math challenges).

- Create a school-wide problem-solving bulletin board to highlight exemplary samples of student work across all grade levels.

- Send problem-solving tips home in a parent newsletter or post them on a school website.

- Inventory supplies and manipulatives in your building and find a system for sharing them among colleagues.

- Hold a problem-solving family math night or discuss the importance of problem solving at your school's Back-to-School Night.

- Begin a problem-solving book study group or focus group for teachers in your school.

Working to Refine Our Skills

Many of us had minimal experience with math problem solving when we were students in the math classroom. Many adults report that they rarely discussed problems, were not taught strategies, learned math skills in isolation, and focused on computations rather than problem solving. While we recognize the importance of problem solving and the need to support our students with problem-solving experiences, it can be challenging to change instructional approaches that are deeply rooted in our own past experiences. And to attempt the change on our own can be daunting. In many schools, teachers are recognizing the benefits of working together to develop a model of an effective teacher of math problem solving. Through co-planning, lesson sharing, professional development sessions, and teacher study groups, we are supporting each other as we develop our skills at teaching math problem solving.

Many teachers applaud the benefits of working in teams. Grade level or other planning teams provide teachers with an opportunity to discuss and co-plan instructional activities with colleagues. Team meetings offer a chance to share resources (e.g., materials, lesson plans), or provide a forum to generate lesson ideas. Teachers can work together to develop a problem task to set a context for an upcoming math concept, analyze samples of student work with colleagues, or debrief after problem experiences to share successes and brainstorm ways to avoid difficulties or clarify misunderstandings. Teaming up with other teachers, whether in a formal or informal setting, allows us to share ideas, refine our understandings, and grow as teachers.

CLASSROOM-TESTED TIP

Refining Our Instructional Practices

Our goal, as teachers, is to continue to strengthen our instructional skills to meet the changing needs of our students. To become effective teachers of math problem solving, we are challenged to find ways to expand and refine our skills as we help students develop this critical math process. Try these activities to continue to refine your teaching skills:

- Read a piece of professional literature and reflect on it as you think about your own experiences in the classroom.

- Look carefully at your students' work. Look for evidence of what they know and clues for how you can help them improve their skills.

- Try new techniques and activities and then reflect on what you've tried. If they are not immediately successful, modify the activities, or your delivery of the activities, to find the best approach for your students.

- Find a colleague with whom you can discuss ideas, share experiences, or even observe his or her teaching.

■ When planning math lessons, consider ways to incorporate problem-solving activities related to all of the content standards.

The Role of the Administrator

The school or district administrator plays a key role in the development of teachers' skills. Providing ongoing professional development is a critical responsibility of administrators. Professional development comes in many shapes and sizes. Teachers benefit from workshops on problem-solving approaches in which new ideas are shared or teaching techniques are modeled. Workshops can infuse new ideas into a staff and are most valuable when there are several sessions, each building upon the others and allowing for teacher reflection. Many schools support the viewing of videotaped classroom lessons (either commercial products or informal tapes made within the school) to provide teachers with examples of teaching methods and to stimulate discussion about the techniques and activities presented in the videotaped lessons. Videos allow teachers to view teaching techniques in action.

Faculty study groups have become a very popular form of professional development because of their ongoing format as well as their potential for encouraging reflection about practice. Study groups might take the form of book studies in which teachers select a relevant piece of professional literature to read and discuss with colleagues over a series of meetings, or might simply be groups of teachers that explore a component of instruction (e.g., math problem solving). A group facilitator guides the discussions and encourages teachers to try related activities in their classrooms, bring student work samples to sessions, or share reflections based on their own practice. Study groups place value on teachers' experiences and enhance those experiences through readings and subsequent discussions. Study groups sometimes evolve into inquiry groups in which teachers explore a key question about problem solving or action research groups in which they gather data and discuss their findings.

The school administrator has the ability to set priorities within the building. Through observations of teaching practice, the administrator can monitor and enhance teaching behaviors. Through the selection of topics for faculty meetings or professional development sessions, administrators can show the importance of math problem solving. Through the designation of a school-based math leader, specialist, or coach, administrators can be reassured that math goals will remain a priority and faculty will receive support and encouragement as they work to refine their skills. Through providing opportunities for discussions with colleagues, peer observations, and study groups, administrators can continue to enhance teacher effectiveness.

Meeting the Needs of All Students

Working together in a school-wide effort to enhance students' problem-solving skills requires attention to all students within the school. Discussions should focus on ways to support struggling students, as well as strategies for extending the problem-solving skills of gifted students. Resource teachers and specialists play a key role in school-wide growth. Specialists with expertise in gifted education, learning disabilities, or English language learners can provide valuable insights into ways to modify instruction to meet the specific needs of these students. Having all faculty assembled to discuss possible strategies will allow specialists to offer tips based on their specific knowledge.

Differentiating instruction to meet the needs of all students is critical in the teaching of problem solving. Understanding key thinking skills and problem-solving strategies, and the way these strategies develop from simple to more complex, is fundamental knowledge that allows us to differentiate our instruction. As we observe students' skills and determine their level of understanding, knowledge of the progression of problem-solving skills will allow us to present simple problems for students who are developing foundation skills or extend problems for those who are ready to be challenged.

The Challenge to Educators

The NCTM Problem-Solving Process Standard guides our efforts to redefine our classroom instruction. As the central focus of the mathematics curriculum (NCTM 1989), problem solving deserves focus and attention within our classrooms, and problem-solving experiences must become a part of our daily mathematics practices. Through the development of a positive classroom climate, we allow our students to test their skills and extend their thinking in a safe, comfortable environment that supports risk taking and creative thinking. Through hands-on and visual teaching techniques, we enable our students to explore problem solving and begin to build a repertoire of strategies and skills to allow them to tackle even complex problems. Through think-aloud techniques, we share our thinking to allow students to see into our heads as they try to understand how to think like problem solvers. Through group and partner work, we allow students to verbalize their ideas, hear the ideas of others, and build on their understanding as they consider new ideas. Through a variety of practice activities, our students are able to extend and refine their skills. And through opportunities for students to identify and assess their own thinking strategies (metacognition), we show students the power of understanding their own thinking.

The National Council of Teachers of Mathematics, through their *Principles and Standards* (2000), has provided us with a guide to help our students develop as math problem solvers. Familiarity with the problem-solving process standard, as well as how it relates to the content standards, will help us to effectively integrate our teaching of math problem solving with our teaching of other math skills and concepts. We can support students to understand and apply their content skills and help them develop problem-solving strategies to solve a variety of math problems.

Our goal as math educators is to acquire skills and strategies to help our students grow as mathematical thinkers. We are challenged to experiment with new strategies and techniques within our classroom to allow students to visualize and experience problem-solving situations. We are challenged to encourage students to communicate their ideas, discuss alternate solutions, and monitor their own thinking processes. We are challenged to present new math ideas in problem contexts to allow students to build on their prior understandings through the active exploration of math concepts. We are challenged to stimulate students with thought-provoking, open-ended problems and guide our students toward reasonable solutions. We are challenged to connect students' classroom skills to meaningful real-world tasks, providing students with opportunities to apply their knowledge. We are challenged to create a classroom in which our students investigate, explore, reason, and communicate about problem solving on a daily basis and in which they can grow to become confident and capable problem solvers.

Questions for Discussion

1. What are the benefits of a school-wide focus on math problem solving? How might you help to create a school-wide focus?

2. In what ways can you improve your skills at teaching problem solving?

3. How does a team approach support classroom teachers? In what ways can classroom teachers and specialists work together to support students as they learn to solve problems?

4. What is the role of the school administrator in developing teachers' understanding of the NCTM problem-solving standard? How might all teachers be supported to better understand the teaching of math problem solving?

Additional Resources for Problem Solving

The following resources are meant to support you as you continue to explore the problem-solving standard in prekindergarten through grade 2. You will find a variety of text resources—books that will provide you with additional problem-solving activities or instructional strategies. A list of math websites is included to supply you with problem tasks, electronic manipulative ideas, or teacher resources. And for additional professional development, several video products are listed that allow you to view problem solving in classrooms and reflect on the video lessons, alone or with a group of your colleagues.

Text Resources

The following text resources provide a variety of activities and strategies for supporting students as they develop their problem-solving skills:

AIMS. 1987. *Primarily Bears— Grades K–6*. Fresno, CA: AIMS Education Foundation.

Burns, M., and B. Tank. 1988. *A Collection of Math Lessons from Grades 1 Through 3*. New York: Math Solutions.

———. 1992. *About Teaching Mathematics*. New York: Math Solutions.

Burns, M., and S. Sheffield. 2004. *Math and Literature: Grades K–1*. Sausalito, CA: Math Solutions.

Charles, R. I., and E. A. Silver, eds. 1989. *The Teaching and Assessing of Mathematical Problem Solving*. Reston, VA: National Council of Teachers of Mathematics.

Coates, Grace Davila, and Jean Kerr Stenmark. 1997. *Family Math for Young Children*. Berkeley, CA: Lawrence Hall of Science.

Coburn, T. G. 1993. *NCTM Addenda Series—Patterns*. Reston, VA: National Council of Teachers of Mathematics.

Findell, C., M. Cavanagh, L. Dacey, C. Greenes, L. Jensen Sheffield, and M. Small. 2004. *Navigating Through Problem Solving and Reasoning in Grade 1*. Reston, VA: National Council of Teachers of Mathematics.

Greenes, C., L. Dacey, M. Cavanagh, C. Findell, L. Jensen Sheffield, and M. Small. 2004. *Navigating Through Problem Solving and Reasoning in Prekindergarten–Kindergarten.* Reston, VA: National Council of Teachers of Mathematics.

Hogeboom, S., and J. Goodnow. 1987. *The Problem Solver I Series.* Mountain View, CA: Creative Publications.

Lester, F. K., and R. I. Charles, eds. 2003. *Teaching Mathematics Through Problem Solving: Prekindergarten–Grade 6.* Reston, VA: National Council of Teachers of Mathematics.

Miller, E. 1998. *Read It! Draw It! Solve It!* Menlo Park, CA: Dale Seymour.

National Council of Teachers of Mathematics. 1989. *Curriculum and Evaluation Standards for School Mathematics.* Reston, VA: National Council of Teachers of Mathematics.

———. 1991. *Professional Standards for Teaching Mathematics.* Reston, VA: National Council of Teachers of Mathematics.

———. 1995. *Assessment Standards for School Mathematics.* Reston, VA: National Council of Teachers of Mathematics.

———. 2000. *Principles and Standards for School Mathematics.* Reston, VA: National Council of Teachers of Mathematics.

———. 2006. *Curriculum Focal Points for Prekindergarten through Grade 8 Mathematics.* Reston, VA: Author.

O'Connell, S. 1997. *Glyphs! Data Communication for Primary Mathematicians.* Columbus, OH: Frank Schaffer Publications.

———. 2001. *Math—The Write Way (Grades 2–3).* Columbus, OH: Frank Schaffer Publications.

———. 2005. *Now I Get It: Strategies for Building Confident and Competent Mathematicians, K–6.* Portsmouth, NH: Heinemann.

Small, M., L. Jensen Sheffield, M. Cavanagh, L. Dacey, C. Findell, and C. Greenes. 2004. *Navigating through Problem Solving and Reasoning in Grade 2.* Reston, VA: National Council of Teachers of Mathematics.

Trafton, P., and D. Thiessen. 1999. *Learning Through Problems: Number Sense and Computational Strategies.* Portsmouth, NH: Heinemann.

Van de Walle, J. A., and L. H. Lovin. 2005. *Teaching Student-Centered Mathematics, Grades K–3.* Pearson Education: New York.

Westley, J. 1994. *Puddle Questions.* Mountain View, CA: Creative Publications.

Web Resources

The following websites provide a variety of lesson ideas, classroom resources, and ready-to-use problem-solving tasks:

www.abcteach.com/directory/basics/math/problem_solving/—The abcteach website has problem-solving activities from PreK through 8th grade. Some are free; others require site membership.

www.aimsedu.org/index.html—This AIMS (Activities Integrating Mathematics and Science) website includes sample activities, information on AIMS professional development, an online store, and other teacher resources.

www.etacuisenaire.com—This website showcases the products of the ETA/Cuisenaire Company, a supplier of classroom mathematics manipulatives and teacher resource materials.

www.heinemann.com—This website of Heinemann Publishing Company provides a variety of professional development resources for teachers.

www.illuminations.nctm.org—Explore a variety of problem-based lessons on this website of the National Council of Teachers of Mathematics.

www.learner.org/channel/courses/teachingmath/gradesk_2/session_03/index.html—This Annenberg Media site offers a free, self-paced online course to help primary teachers better understand the problem-solving standard, including lesson excerpts, video clips, and reflection questions.

www.learningresources.com—This website showcases the products of the Learning Resources Company, supplier of a variety of mathematics manipulatives and teacher resource materials.

www.mathcats.com/storyproblems/housecat2.html—This website contains story problems written by students and interactive math problem-solving activities.

www.mathstories.com—The "House of Math Word Problems" contains problems at the elementary level in both English and Spanish. There is a fee to subscribe.

www.nctm.org—On this National Council of Teachers of Mathematics (NCTM) website you will find information on regional and national conferences sponsored by NCTM, as well as a variety of professional development materials.

www.tomsnyder.com—This Tom Snyder Productions website sells commercial problem-solving software products listed by grade level.

www.wits.ac.za/ssproule/pow.htm—This problem-of-the-week website lists links to problem-of-the-week sites at all academic levels and includes a site rating system.

Staff Development Training Videos

The following professional development training videos feature a problem-solving focus for teaching mathematics and offer tips and strategies for the teaching of math problem solving. These video programs allow teachers to view problem solving in action in primary classrooms. The accompanying manuals provide reflection questions and activity ideas.

Hersch, S., A. Cameron, M. Dolk, and C. Twomey Fosnot. 2004. *Fostering Children's Mathematical Development: Grades PreK–3 (Resource Package)*. Portsmouth, NH: Heinemann.

Mathematics: Teaching for Understanding. 1989. Vernon Hills, IL: ETA Cuisenaire.

Using Vocabulary and Writing Strategies to Enhance Math Learning, Grades 1–2. 2005. Bellevue, WA: Bureau of Education and Research.

Brenner, M. 2000. *Stacks of Trouble*. New York: The Kane Press.

Burns, M. 1992. *About Teaching Mathematics*. Sausalito, CA: Math Solutions.

Carle, E. 1972. *Rooster's Off To See the World*. New York: Scholastic.

Carpenter, T. P., M. L. Franke, and L. Levi. 2003. *Thinking Mathematically*. Portsmouth, NH: Heinemann.

Chambers, D, ed. 2002. *Putting Research Into Practice in the Elementary Grades*. Reston, VA: National Council of Teachers of Mathematics.

Charles, R. I., and E. A. Silver, eds. 1989. *The Teaching and Assessing of Mathematical Problem Solving*. Reston, VA: National Council of Teachers of Mathematics.

Christelow, E. 1989. *Five Little Monkeys Jumping on the Bed*. New York: Clarion Books.

Coburn, T. G. 1993. *NCTM Addenda Series—Patterns*. Reston, VA: National Council of Teachers of Mathematics.

Dee, R. 1988. *Two Ways to Count to Ten*. New York: Henry Holt & Co.

deRubertis, B. 1999. *A Collection for Kate*. New York: Kane Publishing.

———. 1999. *Count on Pablo*. New York: The Kane Press.

Driscoll, L. 2005. *Super Specs*. New York: The Kane Press.

Economopoulis, K. 1998. "What Comes Next? The Mathematics of Pattern in Kindergarten." *Teaching Children Mathematics* 5(4): 230–33.

Ehlert, L. 1992. *Fish Eyes*. New York: Voyager Books.

Ernst, L. C. 1995. *Up to Ten and Down Again*. New York: HarperTrophy.

Ferrini-Mundy, J., G. Lappan, and E. Phillips. 1997. "Experiences with Patterning." *Teaching Children Mathematics* 3(6): 282–88.

Hiebert, J., T. Carpenter, E. Fennema, K. Fuson, D. Wearne, H. Murray, A. Olivier, and P. Human. 1997. *Making Sense: Teaching and Learning Mathematics with Understanding*. Portsmouth, NH: Heinemann.

Hutchins, Pat. 1989. *The Doorbell Rang*. New York: HarperTrophy.

Kassirer, S. 2001. *What's Next, Nina?* New York: The Kane Press.

Kilpatrick, J., W. G. Martin, and D. Schifter, eds. 2003. *A Research Companion to Principles and Standards for School Mathematics*. Reston, VA: National Council of Teacher of Mathematics.

Lester, F., and R. Charles, eds. 2003. *Teaching Mathematics Through Problem Solving: Prekindergarten–Grade 6*. Reston, VA: National Council of Teachers of Mathematics.

Maccarone, G. 1995. *Monster Math*. New York: Scholastic.

Merriam, E. 1993. *12 Ways to Get to 11*. New York: Simon and Schuster Books.

Murphy, S. J. 1998. *Animals on Board.* New York: HarperCollins.

———. 2000. *Beep Beep, Vroom Vroom!* New York: Harper Collins.

———. 2001. *Safari Park.* New York: HarperCollins.

National Council of Teachers of Mathematics. 1989. *Curriculum and Evaluation Standards for School Mathematics.* Reston, VA: Author.

———. 1991. *Professional Standards for Teaching Mathematics.* Reston, VA: Author.

———. 1995. *Assessment Standards for School Mathematics.* Reston, VA: Author.

———. 2000. *Principles and Standards for School Mathematics.* Reston, VA: Author.

———. 2006. *Curriculum Focal Points for Prekindergarten through Grade 8 Mathematics.* Reston, VA: Author.

O'Connell, S. 2005. *Now I Get It: Strategies for Building Confident and Competent Mathematicians K–6.* Portsmouth, NH: Heinemann.

Polya, G. 2004. *How To Solve It: A New Aspect of Mathematical Method,* 3rd ed. Princeton, NJ: Princeton University Press.

Recht Penner, L. 2000. *Clean Sweep Campers.* New York: The Kane Press.

Silver, E. A., and M. S. Smith. 2002. "Teaching Mathematics and Thinking." *Putting Research Into Practice in the Elementary Grades.* Reston, VA: National Council of Teachers of Mathematics (pp. 63–67).

Sowder, L. 2002. "Story Problems and Students' Strategies." In *Putting Research into Practice in the Elementary Grades.* Reston, VA: National Council of Teachers of Mathematics (pp. 21–23).

Stenmark, J. K., ed. 1991. *Mathematics Assessment—Myths, Models, Good Questions, and Practical Suggestions.* Reston, VA: National Council of Teachers of Mathematics.

Trafton, P.R. and D. Thiessen. 1999. *Learning Through Problems.* Portsmouth, NH: Heinemann.

Van de Walle, J. A. 2004. *Elementary and Middle School Mathematics: Teaching Developmentally.* New York: Pearson Education.

Van de Walle, J. A., and L. H. Lovin. 2005. *Teaching Student-Centered Mathematics, Grades K–3.* Pearson Education: New York.

Walsh, E. S. 1991. *Mouse Count.* New York: Harcourt Brace & Co.

Wise, W. 1993. *Ten Sly Piranhas.* New York: Scholastic.

Why Are Student Activities on a CD?

At first glance, the CD included with this book appears to be a collection of teaching tools and student activities, much like the activities that appear in many teacher resource books. But rather than taking a book to the copier to copy an activity, the CD allows you to simply print off the desired page on your home or work computer. No more standing in line at the copier or struggling to carefully position the book on the copier so you can make a clean copy. And with our busy schedules, we appreciate having activities that are classroom ready and aligned with our math standards.

You may want to simplify some tasks or add complexity to others. The activities on the CD often include several parts or have added challenge extensions. When it is appropriate for your students, simply delete these sections for a quick way to simplify or shorten the tasks. Here are some examples of ways you may want to change the tasks and why. A more complete version of this guide with more samples for editing the activities can be found on the CD-ROM.

Editing the CD to Motivate and Engage Students

Personalizing Tasks or Capitalizing on Students' Interests

The editable feature of the CD provides a quick and easy way to personalize math problems. Substituting students' names, the teacher's name, a favorite pet, an up-coming holiday, or a special school event can immediately engage students. You know the interests of your students. Mentioning their interests in your problems is a great way to increase their enthusiasm for the activities. Think about their favorite activities and simply substitute their interests for those that appear in the CD tasks.

In the second version of the following task, the teacher knows that many of his students have never been to a county fair, so he modifies the task. The school just had a carnival, so he uses that context to pose the same math problem. Using the editable CD feature, he makes simple changes to the problem task to create a version of the problem that works well for his students.

Note: This type of editing is important when the problem situation may not be culturally appropriate for your students. It may be that they have no previous experience with county fairs and would not understand this prompt. Substituting an experience that makes sense for your students will make the problem relevant to them.

Name _____

The County Fair

Rita went to the county fair. She used half of her tickets to ride the carousel. Then, she used 3 tickets to ride the bumper cars. She didn't have any more tickets. How many tickets did she have at the start?

_____ tickets

Show your work.

Tell how you got the answer.

_____

_____

_____

_____

Challenge: Tickets cost 10 cents each. How much did Rita have to pay for her tickets? Tell how you know.

May be copied for classroom use. © 2007 by Susan O'Connell from *Introduction to Problem Solving: Grades PreK–2* (Portsmouth, NH: Heinemann).

Name _____

The School Carnival

Rita went to the school carnival. She used half of her tickets to play the bean bag toss. Then, she used 3 tickets to get a grab bag. She didn't have any more tickets. How many tickets did she have at the start?

_____ tickets

Show your work.

Tell how you got the answer.

_____

_____

_____

Challenge: Tickets cost 10 cents each. How much did Rita have to pay for her tickets? Tell how you know.

May be copied for classroom use. © 2007 by Susan O'Connell from *Introduction to Problem Solving: Grades PreK–2* (Portsmouth, NH: Heinemann).

Editing the CD to Differentiate Instruction

Modifying the Readability of Tasks

Adding some fun details can generate interest and excitement in story problems, but you might prefer to modify some problems for students with limited reading ability. While the problem in the second version that follows is the same as in the first version, the task is written in a simpler way to support those students who might benefit from fewer and simpler words. Simply deleting some of the words on the editable form will result in an easy-to-read version of the same task.

Name _____

The Picnic

Annie went on a picnic with her family.

Annie's mother baked 7 cupcakes. Annie ate 2 cupcakes. How many cupcakes were left?

_____ cupcakes were left

Annie put 6 grapes on her plate. She put 3 strawberries on her plate. How many pieces of fruit did she put on her plate?

_____ pieces of fruit

Name _____

The Picnic

There were 7 cupcakes. Annie ate 2 of them. How many were left?

_____ cupcakes were left

Annie had 6 grapes. She had 3 berries. How many pieces of fruit did she have?

_____ pieces of fruit

Creating Shortened or Tiered Tasks

While many students are able to move from one task to another, some students benefit from focusing on one task at a time. By simply separating parts of a task, either by cutting the page into two parts or by using the editable CD feature to put the two parts of the task on separate pages, teachers can help focus students on the first part of the task before moving them to the second part. Teachers might choose to provide all students with the first part and then give students the second part after they have completed the first part and had their work checked by the teacher. In this sample, the two parts of the task, which initially appeared on one page together, are separated. Note that the spaces for student work were enlarged for students who might need additional space, and the challenge task was deleted.

Name _____

Tasty Cookies

1. Janet had a plate of cookies.
   She had the same number of chocolate as sugar.
   She had 4 sugar cookies.
   How many chocolate cookies were on Janet's plate?

   Show your work.

   Janet had _____ chocolate cookies.

2. Eddie had a plate of cookies.
   He had twice as many lemon as oatmeal.
   He had 3 oatmeal cookies.
   How many lemon cookies were on Eddie's plate?

   Show your work.

   Eddie had _____ lemon cookies.

Challenge: Who had more cookies, Janet or Eddie? Tell why.

Name _____

Tasty Cookies

1. Janet had a plate of cookies.
   She had the same number of chocolate as sugar.
   She had 4 sugar cookies.
   How many chocolate cookies were on Janet's plate?

   Show your work.

   Janet had _____ chocolate cookies.

Name _____

More Tasty Cookies

Eddie had a plate of cookies.
   He had twice as many lemon as oatmeal.
   He had 3 oatmeal cookies.
   How many lemon cookies were on Eddie's plate?

   Show your work.

   Eddie had _____ lemon cookies.

Modifying Data

While all students may work on the same problem task, modifying the problem data will allow teachers to create varying versions of the task. Using the editable forms, you can either simplify the data or insert more challenging data.

In the second version that follows, the details were altered with the addition of more coins to create a problem with a bit more complexity. Whether you decide to simply change the numbers in the problem, or slightly alter the other problem information, the editable feature of the CD will allow you to create various versions of the original activity.

Name _____

Carol's Coins

Carol had 2 dimes and 4 nickels. How much money did she have?

Carol had _____ cents.

Show your work.

Tell how you got your answer.

_____

_____

_____

_____

_____

Challenge: If Carol found a quarter, how much money would she have altogether? Tell how you got your answer.

Name _____

Carol's Coins

Carol had 2 quarters, 3 dimes and 4 nickels. How much money did she have?

Carol had _____ cents.

Show your work.

Tell how you got your answer.

_____

_____

_____

_____

Challenge: If Carol found a quarter and a dime, how much money would she have altogether? Tell how you got your answer.